BURNOUT

Renewal in the Wilderness

R. Loren Sandford

p 20 the difference between anointing and natural strength

D1510863

Copyright 1998, R. Loren Sandford
Published by **EXANIMO CORPORATION**
104 Baker River Road
P.O. Box 1110
Concrete, Washington 98237

Copyright © 1998
R.Loren Sandford

All rights reserved. No part of this book may be
reproduced in any form, except for the inclusion
of brief quotations in a review, without permission
in writing from the author or publisher.

ISBN: 1-57502-921-9

Library of Congress Catalog Card Number: 98-93452

Printed in the USA by

MORRIS PUBLISHING

3212 East Highway 30 • Kearney, NE 68847 • 1-800-650-7888

TABLE OF CONTENTS

INTRODUCTION

My first book on burnout was published in 1987, eleven years ago at this writing. I omit the title because it's now out of print. However, over the years, I have received many letters of thanks, often with the statement, "Your book saved my ministry!" That first work was, and remains, one I'm proud of. It was a good book on burnout and stress management, but only that, and I'm glad it's in retirement. Burnout: Renewal in the Wilderness became necessary simply because I grew up some. Time and the hand of God are wonderful teachers!

As I wrote that first book focusing on burnout, I actually thought I was describing what people like St. John of the Cross and St. Theresa of Avila called the "dark night of the soul", but only a young fool would think so - and, though I didn't know it at the time - that is what I was. Those were painful years, more painful than any I had experienced up to that time. But as painful as they were, the dark night of the soul is a much more profound experience than the suffering brought on by burnout, and much more difficult to address.

Unlike burnout, the dark night cannot be repaired through corrective action. It is not a wound from which we heal. Neither corrective measures nor changes in lifestyle can alleviate its symptoms until the wilderness has fully accomplished its purpose. Although the Lord may use external circumstances to accomplish His inner purposes, the dark night involves issues of the heart and spirit that are quite independent of what is going on in the outer world.

The first part of this new book is therefore really about changes in behavior and lifestyle, how to regain control when life and its demands have spun out of control. Behavioral changes effectively alleviate the symptoms of burnout and work to facilitate recovery. They can help restore strength and enable a wounded one to continue with ministry, labor and life. But I know now that my personal experience with burnout served only to soften me up for what God really had in store. It began the breaking of the denial systems and structures of performance I had built over a lifetime to protect a set of roots and fears I had acquired so early in life as to forget they were there. I did experience two good years of recovery from burnout, but the real work had yet to begin.

As opposed to burnout, the dark night of the soul is a time of suffering and loss sent by the hand of God to deal with the deep reaches of our nature and character, even those we had forgotten or that we thought were already well-sanctified. It looks and feels different than burnout and it demands a different set of responses. During the burnout years, I learned what some of those responses should be, got them right, built them into my character and wrote about them in published works. I know now that I had only experienced a rehearsal of traits and responses that would later be tested to their limit.

Some have thought me courageous for baring so much of my soul and my life in such a public way as I did in that first book and the two or three magazine articles that followed it. I'll bare a little more here, but I would respond to such affirmations by asking, "What courage? What is there to hide? What is there to lose that I have not already lost?" I don't mean these questions as a complaint or as an expression of sarcasm. I ask them rhetorically, from a place of rest brought about by the experience of the dark night.

In the end, what really matters besides Jesus? If that sounds trite, understand that what once seemed like trite simplicity has taken on a whole new depth of meaning for me. Maintaining an acceptable public persona in false honor consumes a lot of energy. I no longer have it to spend, and it really is as simple as the person of Jesus. One of my current church members recently commented that my willingness to share my experience of brokenness is evidence of humility, but I have never considered myself a humble man. The long and the short of my motivation for self-disclosure is that my life experience should help others understand their own experiences. If that happens, it's enough for me.

What I say concerning the purposes of God in the wilderness - or the dark night of the soul - may be threatening to some who make no room in their theology for redemptive suffering, but I didn't write this book to start a debate nor will I engage in one. It's enough to say that those who've lived what I describe will understand my message and, I hope, take heart for the outcome of their own walks.

I have written briefly and sought an easy reading style, knowing that those worn down by deep suffering usually have little patience or energy for long books or extended scholarly presentations. I wanted this book to be both accessible and comprehensible to those who suffer most deeply. I hope and pray it provides the encouragement I intend because there's precious little out there. The body of Christ still doesn't deal well with those who suffer for extended periods of time.

I suspect that the great majority of pastors, and even of high-profile lay leaders in our local churches, have at some time experienced a depth of wounding or burnout that has threatened not only their capacity to minister, but even their ability to deal with daily life. Few counselors, much less the body of Christ at large, truly understand the problem because they haven't lived it. As the old saying goes, "It takes one to know one." But God does have answers. Scripture does speak to the issue in ways both healing and true.

Both burnout and the dark night of the soul take a frightening toll on physical health and well-being. Sufferers have often visited the family doctor for any number of associated physical symptoms and have been given a clean bill of health. They leave discouraged and confused because the aches, pains and ills they experience are very real and truly do hinder their ability to function adequately. It's just that medical science has no means of measuring them until catastrophic breakdown threatens.

The "faith", "success in life", and "word of faith" teachings that hang on so stubbornly in our Christian sub-culture are cruel medicine to the burnout victim who already feels as if he/she is failing. To the one in the dark night of the soul these teachings are so beyond irrelevance as to seem

4

laughable, even puerile. Those for whom I write have often reached such a point of emotional and physical weakness that they are unable to accomplish what these performance-oriented teachings call them to perform, no matter how much they try. They simply cannot "believe" any longer or "confess" as they ought and they are therefore often consumed by an overwhelming sense of failure and the guilt that rises from it.

In the end, these teachings only make them feel accused. They're often filled with fear that their fatigue, anxiety, failure and pain will be exposed and condemned, and so they keep to themselves in a dangerous form of withdrawal that invites disaster on a number of fronts. These teachings, although offered in innocence and with a genuine desire to help, often have a way of visiting crippling condemnation on those who really need a deep dose of mercy for their fatigue, anxiety and pain. Their faith has been shaken to the core, and often shattered. They're exhausted spiritually, emotionally and physically and can no longer lift themselves out of the depths by any personal effort at right thinking or acting. Some have despaired even of the knowledge that God truly loves them.

The deeply wounded can no longer find their answers in method. If they need a theology preached to them, it must be a compassionate one that makes sense of redemptive suffering, not a performance-oriented system of religious thought laced with condemnation for failure. A special kind of mercy and grace is called for. Some need simply to be lifted and carried in a tender way that gives much

5

and asks little.

Not infrequently, inner pressures of hurt and despair combine with the continuing demands of ministry, and of dealing with day to day life, to produce a devastating breakdown. Rather than respond with restorative compassion, the body of Christ too often beats the wounded one to death with religious platitudes and back-stabbing suspicions. Years ago I heard a friend of mine say that the body of Christ is the only army in the world that shoots its wounded. How true! Please God, let us develop compassionate understanding for the human weaknesses and needs of those in leadership positions in the body of Christ!

To those teetering on the brink, wounded and fearful, both clergy and lay leaders, I want to say that you are not alone, that you are not hopeless and that God has a merciful plan to move you purposefully through the wilderness and into your promised land. *You have not lost your anointing. You are not rejected. Your ministry is not over.* You may not discern the good goal God has for you, but our Lord is moving you toward it.

I've found the material in this book to be helpful to both clergy and lay folk and to as many as are deeply affected by stress or despair, no matter what walk of life they occupy. Anyone who has suffered long term stress from any cause will find something useful here. I speak from the perspective of a ministry professional, but the symptoms of burnout and of the wilderness experience are the same at any level of calling, whatever the cause.

During my time of burnout there were many

who carried my burden. To them I express my gratitude, especially to those who were then the elders of Cornerstone Christian Fellowship in Post Falls, Idaho, which I planted and pastored for eleven years before leaving in 1991. I've been gone a long time and they are all scattered now, but they supported me in my weakness and carried more than their share of the load while I walked the path of the wounded. I fear some of them are still recovering from the casualty list for the pressure I placed on them. Wherever you are, brothers and sisters, thank you. May the hand of God find you and overflow the vessels of your lives with blessing and goodness.

For support during the time of my walk through the dark night of the soul I especially thank the angel the Lord sent to be my life's partner. Beth's gentle nature and stubborn joy are major reasons I came safely through it all with the changes God intended to make in me. She understood the value of listening, and she sacrificed herself and her personal needs to enable my process. She saw the outcome long before I could sense it and she quietly believed through all the long days and years. God has rewarded her with the man she saw in me in the spirit before we married twenty-five years ago.

Finally, I realize that both women and men suffer in the ways I describe in this book, and for the same reasons. I do, however, find "inclusive language" insufferably tedious. Please realize, therefore, that most of my uses of the masculine pronoun include the feminine. Maybe I'm just a forty-six year old dinosaur, but bear with me, OK? Enjoy.

SOMEWHERE

I hurl my questions high and sing into forever
I wait for answers why
Sometimes it seems like never
Somewhere light glows
Somewhere love flows
And there's a place where the air is clear
A place of wind in the angel's hair
It's gonna be all right
Somewhere tears dry
Somewhere, dreams fly.

I hear the sound of a rushing wind
To fan the flames on our heads again
It's gonna be all right
I hurl my questions high and sing into forever
I wait for answers why
Sometimes it seems like never
and then....
Somewhere light glows
Somewhere love flows
And there's a place where the air is clear
A place of wind in the angel's hair
It's gonna be all right.

PART I

BURNOUT

1
THREE KINDS OF DAMAGE

Burnout has become a common term in the last decade or so. Its use is reflective of a heightened awareness, perhaps even desperation, concerning a widespread problem common among those who expend themselves in the service of others. In my view, this condition actually involves three kinds of damage, of which burnout is only one. Depression and wounding are the other two. I address them because we cannot hope to understand what is happening in what we call burnout without an awareness that we are dealing with damage at several levels, each feeding into and affecting the others.

For the present purpose I'll differentiate burnout from depression and wounding by saying that burnout happens only to givers. Its nature is the depletion of the physical and emotional resources that enable the giver to keep giving. The depletion of these resources leads to despair, depression, irrational anger and a host of physical problems. "Burnouts" are those who have too little consciousness of - or care for - their personal needs to do what is necessary to replenish themselves from the intensity of their giving. The cause of this failure may be a root in performance orientation, or it may be as simple as living through one of those inevitable seasons of high demand experienced by all of us who minister. In either case, a period of rest is often all that is needed to cure simple burnout; the same is seldom true of depression and wounding.

Depression is an emotional manifestation of the

depletion of one's physical and emotional resources for dealing with stress and can happen to anyone, giver or not, who faces unrelenting stress over a period of time and cannot or will not adequately process it. In its most extreme form, depression may be so debilitating that the victim almost completely loses the ability to function and cannot in any way summon up enough initiative to get moving with life again. For such people, hopelessness has become their total environment.

Depression is often the result of performance orientation. Performance-oriented people have not learned that they are acceptable apart from what they can achieve. For the performance-oriented person, the hope of love and the ability to accept oneself always center about the effort to successfully meet the expectations of self or others for behavior or productivity. Unfortunately, this fear motivation for living and achieving exacts a terrible physical and emotional toll. The result can be deep depression until the victim learns that self-acceptance, the love of God and the love of others come by grace, and are totally unearned.

Wounding is an emotional condition, a form of stress, caused by the hurtful acts of others. I've learned that just as the body has finite and exhaustible physical resources it draws upon in order to cope with life, so our emotions tap into limited resources in human strength in order to meet and deal with the lumps life serves up for the heart. When those resources are spent, the result is devastation and desperation. Anyone can suffer emotional wounding, but the wounding is especially severe for those who are givers by nature or by profession.

For those involved in giving professions, it simply won't do, at this point, to talk about professional detachment. In order for us to minister healing, we must risk ourselves. There must be a meeting of persons, and in any meeting of persons there is a necessary level of vulnerability for both parties. Therefore, when one for whom you have poured forth your life turns on you with fangs bared, the pain can be excruciating and the expenditure of emotional energy required to process it can be enormous.

Normally, life serves up its hurts, losses, betrayals and abandonments by loved ones at a pace that leaves time for recovery and replenishment, but occasionally they come either too quickly, or they wound us too deeply, for us to recover effectively before the next onslaught. The result is wreckage in the form of physical illness, depression, withdrawal, paranoia and fear of emotional risk.

Obviously, there are significant areas of overlap and interrelationship between burnout, depression and wounding, both in causes and effects. I have differentiated between burnout, wounding and depression in this chapter only to emphasize that the condition I'm ultimately addressing is more serious and more complex than the kind of thing many of us have become accustomed to reading about in professional journals or even in books on the subject.

The pain suffered by so many is clearly deeper than can be accounted for by the mere depletion of energies. Likewise, the remedies often involve much more than just rearranging schedules and prioritizing activities. Having made this point, I will henceforth use the terms "burnout", "wounding" and their derivatives interchangeably.

For the sake of discussion, I have divided the process of degeneration into three stages. Each of these stages of burnout, in turn, is examined in three sections: the first describing the physical symptoms evident at that stage, the second addressing the emotional condition of the sufferer and the third suggesting what sort of ministry can be appropriately offered by those who wish to help.

2
Stage One Burnout:
<u>ONSET</u>

Physical Symptoms

In the early stages of wounding or burnout, the sufferer may feel chronic fatigue and noticeably increased recovery times following severe exertions of time and energy. In ministry, crises such as funerals, conflicts or even commitments requiring extra time (like week-long summer camps or conferences) begin to require discouragingly long periods of time for recovery. Whereas the individual may have recovered quickly in the past from the kind of extra energy expenditures that ministry demands from time to time (a couple of days sleeping in, perhaps), he now needs a week or more to feel really right again.

Tired people make more mistakes than healthy ones. Thought processes slow down. Perceptions of reality may become distorted. Reactions to events are less well-considered. As one in the early stages of burnout grows more fatigued, errors, especially in relationships with others, inevitably multiply. This will most directly affect sensitive relationships that are important to maintain for the health of the ministry or the balance of a life. Vital support systems are often seriously damaged by these mistakes.

One brother who held a key position in our church had a history of financial struggles. In our first year as a church in Idaho, we were discussing some enormous need that required a lot of money in order to meet it. I knew we didn't have it. He persisted until I blurted, "This is from a man who has filed bankruptcy?!" hoping to joke or tease him off the subject. Bad joke! I instantly flushed hot with shame. Under normal circumstances I would never have let myself say anything so stupid and ill-considered, much less allow a hurtful word to come out of my mouth. It took a long time to repair the damage. I was too tired, and as a result, I wounded someone I cared about.

Because the burnout victim, even in the early stages, sometimes fails to hear things that are said to him through the veil of his fatigue, he may occasionally respond inappropriately to those who come to him with questions and needs. He may mean to tease a friend in a loving way, but it comes out sounding like a hurtful insult. He may forget to include important people in the plans he makes for the ministry and then have to suffer their sense of rejection and/or their wrath for his error.

All of this opens the door to the critical spirit that continually seeks opportunity to exert itself in any fellowship, in the church, in an organization or in any web of relationships. Tongues begin to wag and this adds to the burden of stress that has begun to drag the burnout victim down. I've learned that for every person I offend in some way, there is an "army" of twenty to fifty waiting to be secondarily offended as the story is passed around. Some may begin to assign evil motives to the burnout victim's actions, to assail his character and to accuse him of not loving them or of being insensitive to their needs.

Such talk creates a negative spiritual pressure

on the ministry that tends to lock up anointing and to hinder effectiveness. Even Jesus couldn't do many miracles in His own hometown because of the unbelief of the people living there. The burnout sufferer knows more deeply than anyone else the meaning of what Jesus faced.

More and more frequently he doesn't feel good about getting up in the morning. Refreshment eludes him and there are whole days when he feels unexplainably and uncharacteristically sleepy so that he must push himself to keep moving.

Falling asleep at night is increasingly difficult, and rarely is the night restful when he finally does doze off. His mind won't let go of things and it races on, refusing every effort to control it. At first he may pass it off as part of his giftedness, "I do my best creative thinking in bed before I go to sleep." It's probably true, but in reality, it's just a manifestation of performance orientation that renders him unable to let go of things enough to find peace. In the later stages of burnout, creativity will die out, while wakefulness continues tearing at him, night after night. Dreams are increasingly troubled, leaving him exhausted in the morning as if he'd been working all night.

He begins to manifest physical tension reactions. My personal "favorite" is what I call "lockjaw". It's a wonder my teeth survived the pressure. Others may notice increasing and chronic muscle tension in the shoulders or other areas. Unconscious nervous tappings of the hands and feet may appear. Twitching of muscles in the face or elsewhere may become habitual. Headaches may increase in frequency and intensity.

For many of us, tension tends to express itself through the digestive system. Early symptoms of colitis may appear as chronic pain in the lower abdomen, or as recurring bouts with irregularities in bowel movements - or both. Problems with acid indigestion and stomach ulcers may develop.

Emotional Condition

More than anything else, there may be an increasing awareness of vague fear and anxiety - not attributable to any known cause except when it can be attached to a coming situation in which performance is called for. At this stage, such anxiety is still just background noise that can be eclipsed by the intensity of ministry, the warmth of a ministry anointing, adrenalin rush or simply by relentless activity. For many of us such fear may even be an effective tool for enhanced performance because of the slight adrenalin edge it gives, but this benefit will pass. I promise. Such anxiety may be objectively identified as fear of failure, fear of the unknown, fear of attack or any other sort of fear, but my point is that the ability to deal with it, and to subdue it, has begun to erode.

In the early stages of wounding, more and more nagging questions arise concerning one's faith and personal relationship with God which seem to have no satisfactory answers. The early burnout victim asks, "Is the counseling I'm doing really effective? Are people really changed? Will I really receive or achieve the things God has promised me? Will the problems ever be solvable? Is God really here for me?" Yet, in spite of the fear and the questioning, he still hopes deeply and is able to encourage others with that hope. The disturbing thing is that his ability to live creatively with the questions is beginning to weaken.

His prayer life remains intact. Daily devotions are still a source of refreshment and of conversation with God, but he begins to wonder at the frequency and duration of dry times. Perhaps more significantly, fatigue, the pressure of daily life and the demands of people for his personal ministry begin to cut into his prayer time and he feels helpless to stop it. This often happens during what seem to be his greatest periods of growth and anointing. In the glow of success, it's easy to ignore warning symptoms.

At this stage he still has confidence in his ability, anointing and strength - if confidence and strength were what he began his ministry with. My wife warned me repeatedly about the quantity of energy I was expending. I answered, "I have a course to run, Beth, and I don't have God's permission to stop yet. The job isn't done." We were involved in starting a new church, laying foundations, building people and all the intensity of investment that comes with the task of carving a body of Christ out of the spiritual wilderness. On the one hand, I know I was right and that I would say the same thing again. But, on the other hand, I know that the *spirit* of my reply would be different today because the spirit of my effort would be different. No matter how demanding the work might be, there would be a peace in the effort that I couldn't imagine when I was younger.

At this early stage, the anointing of the Lord does sustain you in spite of fatigue, but more and more often you run on adrenalin strength, sometimes not knowing the difference between adrenalin rush and the anointing of God. Understanding the difference is a function of wisdom, and wisdom is won only through time and suffering.

In stage one, the individual entering upon burnout begins to shave such healthy, self-renewing activities as recreation and exercise from his schedule. He may even feel a bit noble about it, glorying in the delusory sense that he is wearing himself out in the service of the Lord. And it's true; he really does love the Lord, but work and its related stresses leave little energy for fun and personal replenishment. The care of his physical "temple" suffers. And our reasons for engaging in such self-destructive behavior are never as pure as we tell ourselves they are.

Time away from work still recharges his batteries and reenergizes his creativity, but he is ever more disturbed at how quickly his physical and emotional reserves dissipate after he returns. He begins to wonder how long he would have to be away in order to come back fully recovered.

Ministry to Stage One

At this point, normal ministry is still possible. A stage one burnout victim can still engage in the kind of interaction with others that is so necessary to most healing. You can talk with him concerning root causes of his condition and he can respond, recognize his sin and pray wonderfully well in relation to it. You can pray for his deliverance and he'll shed tears and thank you for it. As a result, he may make some short-lived attempts to adjust his lifestyle, but don't expect much fruit in the long run. Most likely he already knows what must be done to turn his condition around and either can't or won't do it.

As I was, by this time he's probably locked into a set of self-destructive patterns that are too strong, too pervasive or too cloaked in denial to be easily or quickly broken. He will likely have to ride those patterns to the bottom before the delusion they represent is fully exposed and their power is fully defeated in his life. He'll have to burn out on being burned out.

I myself knew I had a task to perform from which I couldn't turn aside and in which I felt I had too little real help. That much was true, but I was driven by fears of rejection and failure of which I was completely unaware. That combination of pressures prevented me from slowing down long enough to deal with the issue of my own needs in a life-changing way. Real healing was impossible until the course had been run and the task was finished. The finishing nearly killed me and in the end I felt I failed, anyway.

It seems to me that conventional wisdom focuses on preventing burnout from occurring. I'm not certain this is always the wisest approach, or even the will of God. I'm not all that interested in preventing burnout because I'm convinced that the condition can be a tool of the Lord for crucifying His servants unto new life. In fact, sometimes it's the

19

only tool we "blockheads" leave Him to work with.

In burnout, old patterns are burned away, along with old attitudes and fleshly ways of approaching life and its inhabitants. Even had I known how to stop my downward slide in its early stages, I probably wouldn't have done it, because all along I had the mysterious sense that it was the hand of God leading me down this path and that, if I simply embraced the pain, I would learn wisdom. I was right. Jesus is Lord. What I didn't know was how much pain I would ultimately be asked to absorb.

At the time that I began to burn out, I thought I was entering upon what is often known as "the dark night of the soul". Especially if you are a dynamic personality, you begin your ministry filled with talents and abilities and endowed with boundless energy to make those talents and abilities effective in ministry. In the beginning you aren't wise or experienced enough to know the difference between anointing and natural strength, and no matter what you think or acknowledge theologically concerning the sin of man, you really have no idea how far from the nature of Jesus your own character is. But it isn't yet important for you to be fully aware of this because the name of the game at this point is growth and knowledge, as opposed to a holy awareness of your limitations.

Then, just when it seems you have it all together and that everything you touch turns to gold because of the anointing of God on your life and because of the wisdom He's taught you, God takes it all away. Nothing works anymore. God seems far off and you begin to question everything you thought you knew. You can burn out and remain successful. You can burn out and things may still work, at least for a while, but the dark night of the soul takes you beyond burnout and into a darker place. You've been taken to the cross and there is no escape until you know that you have nothing and that He has all, until the flesh is burned away and the Spirit makes you alive. Until that point, all you can do is hold your heart open to the searingly bright light of His presence and endure the pain His purity creates in your flesh and in your brokenness. It won't look like the God you've known. You won't recognize it as light at first, but light it is.

Finally, when you can endure no more, when the cross has done its work, our Lord restores all that you lost, but now it's no longer yours. It's His. And you know it more deeply than you ever thought possible.

I thought burnout was that process of the dark night, but it was only Act One, Scene One. It set the stage for what came later. Burnout weakened me, but it didn't expose my deepest fears and flaws. It didn't fundamentally change me. That was to come later in a real dark night of the soul.

Anyway, I'm not really interested in prevention of burnout because I'm not much interested in preserving the flesh. From start to finish, from burnout to dark night, this is a suffering to be embraced, accepted and seen through to its end. Though he may not know it, the stage one burnout victim is still running hard in his natural strength, and God has set him on a course to bring it to an end.

21

3
Stage Two Burnout
<u>BREAKDOWN BEGINS</u>

Physical Symptoms

Adrenal burnout begins. I'm not a physician. I know only what I'm told by those who care for my body professionally. Adrenal burnout occurs when the adrenal gland has overproduced for such a long time that it can no longer function as it was designed to function. Whereas stress once created an adrenalin "rush" that could be used to enhance performance, it now often produces a sensation of sickness, like trying to start a car in cold weather on a dead battery.

In fact, the sufferer has become stress-addicted. He actually subconsciously needs and creates stressful work situations so that the fear, the pressure and the resulting adrenalin production overcome his fatigue. But adrenalin no longer gets him moving like it once did. The "rush" is gone. More often, now, situations that once produced the energizing rush just make him sick and angry.

For example, from time to time I used to find myself in unexpected possession of a free day for sermon preparation early in the week, but rather than take advantage of it to reduce my stress load, I would almost subconsciously find some way of filling up that free time so that I would be "under the gun" on Saturday. Why? Because I *needed* to be under the gun. "I work better under pressure." Have you heard that one? Those who make that statement are good candidates for burnout. Given a light work load, I produced mediocre work, but given an overload, I worked like a madman at the peak of my form and excellence. I *needed* stress in order to function, and without it, I went to sleep from fatigue. One of the recovering alcoholics in my congregation once asked me if I was addicted to adrenalin flow. I had to answer yes.

At stage two in the process of degeneration, stress addiction begins to fail as a motivator and fatigue is taken for granted as an unpleasant fact of life. Burnout victims then find it difficult to remember, or even to imagine, life without exhaustion.

Digestive disturbances are common, attacking whatever is the weakest link in the system. The wounded one may develop full-blown ulcers. Colitis may flair up, become a settled condition and cause extreme pain. Diarrhea is common. Food allergies may appear. This is because the digestive system reacts to stress by producing more acid and other chemicals than the system was designed to process. The result is that it becomes overly sensitive to minor irritants it might have easily thrown off before stress took its toll.

Not only is sleep occasionally difficult, it becomes a labor. I remember dreaming night after night that I was engaged in a battle in which I had no power over my enemy. Every movement was like swimming through cold molasses, every stroke of sword or fist deprived of force. Or I might find myself in combat without my sword and swinging at my enemy with an imaginary one. I even made swooshing noises to make it seem more real. After a night of fruitless warfare, I would awaken drained and sick. Sleeping became so difficult that I would stay up late, night after night, partly in order to reach such a point of fatigue that I would sleep quickly and soundly.

In general, physical illness becomes more common. Colds come more frequently and stay longer. Aches and pains proliferate mysteriously. Sore throats develop several times each year and take ages to overcome. Headaches increase in frequency and intensity.

The sufferer may notice that his physical tension reactions to ministry situations have intensified. My sinuses would swell shut and my eyes would feel as if they wanted to cross whenever I faced an afternoon of counseling appointments. They'd become so heavy with sleep that I would catch myself nodding off in the midst of someone's tear-filled account of terrible woe and I would cry out desperately to God to please make it end. It was as if I were physically allergic to ministry. I discovered that if I loaded up on caffeine from the coffee pot before I began my counseling day, I could make it through. But that caused negative side effects, too, as well as diminishing returns.

Emotional Condition

Anxiety becomes nearly constant and is harder to ignore. At this stage, the sufferer may be plagued with anxiety that the ministry will fail and that things are going wrong in ways he is powerless to correct. From where will the next blow fall? Betrayals and fears appear larger than life and his perspective is restored only by a major exercise of mental discipline.

For example, I have a burden bearer's nature. I feel the emotions of those around me almost as if they were my own, much like Counselor Troi, the empathic Betazoid on the television series, *Star Trek: The Next Generation.* I can sense in my spirit how our church is doing at any given time, instinctively knowing when there is discord or trouble, even when I'm two thousand miles away on a speaking trip. During the years of burnout, I could sense when poisonous tongues began to wag in the church, and I would be gripped by fear in a way that distorted my perception of reality and that I no longer had the capacity to control. I still had the strength to govern how I responded to it, but I couldn't control its intensity or maintain my balance emotionally.

I sensed when personal attacks were developing and was doubly wounded by them by reason of fear, and of the cognitive distortions that flowed from fear, when those personal attacks materialized. Cognitive distortions made things seem bigger than they really were. I even began to be fearful that my anointing would expire. God never let me down, but I feared just the same. Road trips for speaking engagements around the country became welcome respites from pressure in the home ministry. At home I felt powerless, but in foreign places overwhelmingly positive responses from people restored my flagging sense of anointing.

At last the wounded one's confidence is threatened. He begins to feel as if he is ministering from an empty bucket that isn't being refilled.

Desperation takes root as again and again he goes to the well for strength and wisdom to meet the needs of others and finds little or nothing to draw upon.

As he loses perspective on the significance of failures and setbacks, he finds himself unable to take encouragement from successes as he once did. In fact, he may become functionally blind to the goodness in his ministry and nothing anyone says will be able to alter that perception or keep him on track.

Ministry becomes unrelenting pain, interspersed with brief episodes of joy and sanity. He finds himself growing more and more angry with those who ask for his time and energy, most especially with the ubiquitous church "leeches" who consume vast amounts of time and energy for little apparent return or purpose. The likelihood is that he has never learned the skill of prioritizing which individuals shoult receive his attention. As a result, those leaders and workers who could share the burden with him are neither nurtured nor adequately developed. Other people devour the time.

Episodes of withdrawal and isolation come more and more frequently, with heightened intensity and extended duration. Since he has no energy left with which to deal with demands of any kind, he withdraws even from family and friends. In this condition, even offers of love may seem to him to be demands that he must respond to in some way so that, instead of feeling refreshed by the love of those close to him, he may actually feel drained by it.

People around him in the ministry may add to his wounding by complaining that he doesn't seem as warm as he once did. For example, circumstances may prevent him from being present for a crisis or two. That becomes an occasion for the victims of the crisis to attack him in private conversation because they couldn't understand his absence.

He begins to wonder angrily if his people would be satisfied if he gashed himself and gave them his very blood. What sacrifice would finally be enough? If his normal nature is to be physically affectionate, people may begin to feel that his hugs aren't as real as they once were, if he still gives them at all. It may be apparent that he doesn't listen as well as he used to. All this may provoke negative and critical talk in the fellowship that adds to his burden of stress.

He may begin to stay up late at night more often in order to find time alone. In my own case, having both an acute spiritual awareness and a burden bearing nature, I can feel the people to whom I minister drawing on me spiritually and emotionally until about 10:00 p.m. when they begin to go to bed. At that hour I can actually sense them letting go of me, and by 11:00 p.m. I'm blissfully alone in every way.

When I'm in withdrawal mode, those late night hours become *my* time. But it's a self-defeating pattern because morning doesn't come any later, and my sleep hours are accordingly abbreviated. Others in this condition perhaps go to bed early and get up early for the same reasons. The wounded one feels driven to find that time in solitude.

Episodes of rage at God become common. In fact, one factor differentiating burnout from the dark night of the soul is the presence or absence of anger.

27

The second stage burnout feels abandoned and betrayed by God. In his eyes God hasn't been a protector. God hasn't kept His promises to him and never will. He feels as though God is there for others through him, but seldom for him personally. God has let him down.

In 1980 I planted Cornerstone Christian Fellowship in Post Falls, Idaho from nothing. From the start, God gave us a number of promises for that church concerning growth and ministry, but rather than fulfill them immediately, He gave us a double dose of troublemakers who went right to work attacking me and distorting my every word and action. When they couldn't find something legitimate to distort and magnify, they'd make things up, and along the way they'd convince themselves that what they made up was true. So, until they left the church, we got nowhere as a congregation in terms of realizing the promises of God for us.

Later, I understood what a foundational time that had been and how precious was all the wisdom I learned, but, while it was happening, it didn't seem that way. It seemed then that if the Lord said to make room for all the growth He would give us, the next Sunday would see a record low attendance for the year! Invariably, I felt betrayed, and, at last I became angry.

Because of the betrayals by people and God's delay in fulfilling promises, I experienced episodes of such deep wounding that I began to call God a liar, betrayer and promise-breaker. I asked Him not to promise me anything anymore because I couldn't stand the pain of being let down yet again and again.

Needless to say, prayer life suffers at this stage and becomes a roller-coaster of ups and downs. Sometimes God comes through in prayer with such blessing that you feel like a fool for all the anger you felt. But more and more the prayer closet becomes a place of pain and alienation, a place to remember that God hasn't kept His promises and that He has not protected you from the strife of tongues. As a result, you pray less. The wounded one in stage two can still hope - and does so in blessed episodes of light and freedom - but the ability to do it is fading fast. Periods of despair are common and almost paralyzing.

As emotional control breaks down, he finds himself subject to sudden impulses to weep over silly things. One of the jokes in my family is how I hate children's features like *Winnie the Pooh* or *101 Dalmatians*. My children are grown now, but when they were little, we'd have a friendly family teasing session every time such a movie would come on television and I'd be forced to watch it with the kids. I would try in vain to hide it, but they all learned to look for my tears, to catch me leaking over a bunch of stupid puppies! Greater emotional freedom is one of the lasting legacies of my burnout years.

At this point in my downward slide, I could be found secretly turning on the Disney Channel late at night and sniffling over the sorrows of some ridiculous cartoon character, wondering what on earth was the matter with me. Actually, I had so many stored-up unresolved hurts and tensions that it wasn't hard to tap into them and make them overflow.

Creativity in ministry is affected because there just isn't enough energy, enthusiasm or faith left to think up new things. That builds fear for the future of the work, and the fear only adds to the problem. Creative, artistic temperaments need "down" time in which to recharge, time when the mind is allowed to work at its own pace, unbullied, until it naturally generates something new and fresh. When it does, there is a sense of relief, release and lifting that beats dozens of hours of counseling for the refreshment it brings. Stage two burnout victims find their "down" time invaded and stolen and they feel powerless to stop it. The result is a build-up of tension and anger with no avenue of release.

One's sex life may begin to suffer because emotionally he can no longer function in the give and take of relationships, and because, physically, he's too weak to generate much libido. That can lead to stress in a marriage, which, in turn, adds to the problem. Still others may find tension release in *heightened* sexual activity or even in illicit aberrations like pornography or compulsive masturbation.

Beth and I never stumbled in our marriage, but it was evident that in my withdrawal I wasn't giving her as much affection as I once did, either in public or in private. Beth and I had always enjoyed a happy marriage, and she fully understood where I was, giving me the room to withdraw as I needed. At this point, one of the women in the church took it upon herself to decide how "hurt" Beth was and she attacked me for it. Beth set her straight, but the incident plunged me into all those other fears. The cycle continued to spiral downward.

Ministry to Stage Two

If approached at just the right moment, and in just the right way, a burnout victim at this stage of degeneration can still spill his hurt to another human being and receive ministry, but more than anything else he needs simply to be listened to with a sympathetic ear. He doesn't usually want a solution, and un-asked-for advice may lead to rage and more withdrawal. He knows he wouldn't be able to pursue that advice with his fading energies, and so it only comes to him as more pressure to perform what he is losing the ability to perform. He just needs a safe place to dump the pain until he can recover his strength, or at least until he is able to go on functioning a while longer.

He can still look at roots and causes for his pain in terms of his own hidden sins, but he can do so only at times of his own choosing. In Scripture, Job's comforters were well-intentioned fools trying to convince him that his suffering was due to something for which he needed to repent. They were wrong. Unfortunately the body of Christ today is full of Job's comforters. More than my share of them came to me in my pain to confront me "in love" and to show me that my plight was because of hidden sin. Hidden sin *was* present. It always is. But I couldn't have dealt with it at the time and it was cruelty to demand that I do.

31

It may help a stage two burnout victim if you kidnap him from time to time and take him out for fun, but don't talk ministry when you do. During this period of my life, one man who didn't at that point attend our church, would show up at my door from time to time and ask my wife, "Can Loren come out and play?" He might have a trailer full of go-carts waiting out front, or a movie he wanted to attend. One time, it was motorcycles, which I don't ride well, but enjoyed anyway. Whatever he had up his sleeve, we'd play like kids for a few hours, without uttering a single word about church or ministry. These were healing and holy times from God, designed to restore my balance by rooting me in the good earth.

Intercede in prayer, but mostly at a distance where your burnout victim doesn't have to respond. He'll feel it. Tell him you're praying, but don't tell him too much about what you're specifically asking God to do. He might take it as pressure or responsibility to make your prayers happen, even though you don't mean it that way.

Don't discuss his condition with others. If you do, he'll likely sense it - or hear about it - and it will feed his paranoia. When you encounter others speaking about him in an unclean way, stop them. Don't even answer questions from those who express concern for him, except to say that he can always use prayer from those who love him.

If the Lord gives you a specific Scripture reference or prophecy of hope for him, send it or give it in written form. It will feed his hope. Don't confront him face to face with it, but leave him free to read it and to respond in private where he won't feel responsible to you for his reaction.

Take up the sword on his behalf. If there is warfare in the church, he will treasure, above all, your taking up his cause. I have valued few gifts more than the one the elders at Cornerstone gave me when the battle erupted over changes we made to our by-laws to bring them more into conformity with the Scriptures. The reaction from a small, but vocal, minority was vicious and aimed at me personally. The objections were based on distorted perceptions of what we had enacted, and the opposition immediately turned to name-calling. I was accused of being everything from egomaniacal to cultish. In truth, I was on the edge of collapse after three years of warfare in which I had stood mostly alone.

Up to that time, every time the going got rough, my supporters and team had lapsed into paralysis and abandoned the flock to be devoured by wolves. This time the elders rallied and told me that it was their battle and not mine. That support was more healing to me than anyone could imagine. As a result, the church came through in shining triumph, and God began to fulfill what He had promised for us.

4
Stage Three Burnout
INCAPACITY

Here is the most misunderstood of the three stages of wounding. As our Elijah House team prepared for the seminar on burnout that gave birth to this book, we discussed various roots and causes of wounding. We looked at driving factors like performance orientation, the need for the wounded one to forgive those who betrayed him and actions that could be taken to facilitate recovery. We talked about praying through the hurts that spring from betrayal until peace and resolution come. We examined changes in lifestyle and support systems. I didn't understand why, at first, but as we talked, I grew more and more angry.

Finally, I realized that what we were discussing was good medicine for someone in the earlier stages of burnout, but that it could be dangerously destructive for the deeply wounded, among whom I was a perfect example. The stage three burnout victim can no longer initiate or sustain his own recovery and lives in a daily prison of despair. If we had pursued the course we were planning, we would have driven a number of those present at the seminar into deeper hopelessness and despair because they would have come to the seminar in a state of *incapacity*. Had we gone no further in our discussions, we would have been asking them to do what they had lost the ability to do. We would have failed tragically to address the needs of the incapacitated.

There are those so deeply wounded that they can only be carried, not exhorted or confronted. They need to be loved, not instructed. Many of them have already prayed through all the things listed above. They've examined and re-examined every root in sin they can think of or even imagine, and they've forgiven or repented for all they're aware of. It seems there's nothing left for them to try, but still they hemorrhage emotionally. They know by experience that there are no simple or quick means to the recovery they seek, and this knowledge frightens them.

Part of this despair comes from the fact that the body of Christ is seldom able to get beyond the demand for simplistic and quick fixes. We have been trained to seek instantaneous miracles, especially in charismatic circles, which comprise a major share of my own beloved heritage. But there are no such miracles for the third stage burnout victim and he knows it. In fact, he's frightened by it and so our simplistic solutions to his desperate problem serve only to drive him deeper into incapacity. Please give careful attention to this section, even if some of it offends some personally cherished theological viewpoint. I know what I'm talking about.

Physical Symptoms

A third stage burnout victim feels physically ill every day. He is so worn out, and his physical and spiritual resources so depleted, he feels as if his spirit were installed in his body like a screw with the threads crossed. Physically, he feels slightly poisoned most of the time and suffers continual pain in various parts of his body. The constant flow of adrenalin produced by stress may have eroded the strength of his connective tissues and so there are persistent aches and pains in various joints and ligaments. My shoulders used to hurt so deeply in the connective tissues that no amount of over-the-counter pain killer brought relief. After a while my toe joints began to hurt and occasionally to spasm. I was experiencing back problems and was seeing a chiropractor who complained that my ligaments were so weak that the adjustments he gave me wouldn't hold. Headaches became daily events, often arriving "on schedule" and with such intensity that I occasionally became nauseous. I would take three to five aspirins to ease the pain, only to begin shaking from the overdose of medicine in my system. Lower dosages brought no relief. Painful fluid-filled blisters appeared on the balls of my feet that had nothing to do with physical overuse. They rose from well beneath the skin and were not athlete's foot. As I later recovered from burnout, the blisters disappeared.

Digestive disturbances become a daily experience and it seems that every meal leads to later pain. At this stage, food addictions, weaknesses and allergies are greatly aggravated. My craving for sugar increased at the same time that my physical ability to process it vanished. For those who are stressed out, refined sugar is a poison. Repeatedly, I would compulsively ingest some sugar-laden delight, only to be devastated at the effect produced in my body. No longer was there the sugar "high" followed by the low that healthy people seem to experience. I went directly to the low, as if a toxin were running throughout my system. My eyes felt like they wanted to cross and I could barely stay awake. Sometimes sugar consumption brought on a headache.

Sleep is *never* satisfactory. Every night he may be tormented by difficulty falling asleep. Every morning he wakes up feeling ill. People begin to comment on how bad he looks.

At this point the burnout victim's heart may begin to act up by way of warning him that he must do something quickly to correct his physical and emotional condition. Angina and heart attacks are not uncommon among those predisposed to heart disease. I myself paid a visit to the family doctor because my heart was missing beats and convulsing, sometimes with pain. After running a series of tests, he told me I was experiencing preventricular contractions. In other words, sometimes the ventricles of my heart failed to pump in proper sequence. According to my doctor, it wasn't a dangerous condition, but it was a clear warning. One young man I know began having false heart attacks. He experienced the pain in his chest and arm consistent with heart attack, but his heart was healthy. Again, a warning.

Every other physical symptom listed under stage one and stage two is present, but in amplified form. Breakdown is imminent.

Emotional Condition

For the burnout victim at this stage there is no respite from the sense that God has betrayed him. No divine promise can be relied upon because God has broken them all. There is no protection or help for him in the Lord. He has been utterly abandoned and even "used" by God without regard for his own personal needs. Although he may know intellectually that God loves him, there are almost no moments when he knows this with his heart. These divine betrayals seem devastatingly real. He is trapped in a set of cognitive distortions that block out all light and good in the real world outside. They just don't reach him.

For instance, in my daily devotions God would say to lengthen the tent cords and enlarge the place of meeting because He was going to bring more growth in our church than we could house. The very next Sunday would be a record-low attendance for the year. God would promise me that my people would volunteer freely in the days of our power. There would be a workday on the church property scheduled for the following week and no one would show up.

I began to feel as if God were deliberately setting me up for disappointment just for torment's sake. I didn't want to hear anything from Him anymore because my faith and trust were in tatters and each promise seemed like a set-up for more heartache. Today I see those promises coming true for the church I now pastor, but during that period of time I'd lost my perspective.

Personal prayer life comes to a near standstill because there is nothing in it but pain. If the burnout victim prays at all, he does so in settings where private intimacy with God is not possible. Ironically, he may continue to pray wonderfully in ministry situations because there he can still occasionally feel the anointing and the presence of God, but he often feels betrayed afterward because the Lord doesn't seem to be there for him personally.

The wounded one is all but defenseless against the blows and pressures of daily life. Every breakdown of routine, every failure of others to carry out their tasks as they overlap with his, occasions the deepest depression or even rage. Several times I stopped assigning tasks to others because I could no longer deal with the pain that came from feeling personally let down when the tasks weren't performed. I could no longer risk the emotional devastation that came from my helpers failing me.

No resiliency remains, either emotionally or physically. Any exertion at all becomes extremely painful for every part of body and spirit. The burnout victim in stage three of degeneration feels like a fighter who can no longer ward off his opponent's blows. He can't even hold up his fists anymore. All he can do is resolve to remain in the ring and take it. Had the blows come with enough space between them, he could have caught his breath and remained on top of things, but too many pressures, crises and betrayals have piled one on top of another. There has been no room to recover between the blows and now he is broken.

For the first time in my life I was driven to active hatred. With no time to think and pray through the hurts, pressures and betrayals as they came at me, I felt myself backed into a corner until I had nothing left but rage. The group of persecutors was small, but effective, and the more so because of my fatigue and my unresolved issues of rejection and fear. For my love they returned criticism. For my best counsel they had returned distorted reflections of all I had said, and, to make matters worse, they had enlisted others in the attack. They would say, "He doesn't love us," while I stumbled around, exhausted from being there for them in their emergencies day after day in counsel, often into the wee hours of the morning. The darkness and confusion they generated penetrated even the beauty of our worship and began to drag down the spirit of the entire congregation. Scarcely had the echoes of one incident died out before I'd find myself facing another. My spirituality was stripped bare and I was left with the bitter taste of raw emotion in my mouth. It was a feeling I couldn't control. I'd never consciously hated before.

Every nerve burns. Unless extraordinarily good restraints were built into the character of the wounded one early in his life, then one who has otherwise been kind and loving may suddenly become dangerously explosive in his anger. Even violent. Spouses of such wounded ones may be confused and hurt by violent reactions to what seem to be small requests or insignificant irritants. The wounded one is literally screaming inside with rage and desperation. Gone are the physical resources that enable the mind to fight off insanity or overcome distorted perceptions.

I believe, but cannot substantiate, that there are certain physical resources, chemicals or nutrients, produced and/or stored by the body, which the body then utilizes to combat stress. They enable us to maintain a grip on the whole of reality when certain aspects of reality become painful. Under conditions of prolonged stress these resources are used up and the body has a most difficult time replacing them. As a result, our spiritual, emotional and mental processes break down. Medical science provides very little help at this point because there seems to be no method for measuring what these resources are or how to renew them. The family doctor can only declare that his tests reveal no measurable physical or chemical abnormalities. It's frustrating, because the sufferer knows what physical and emotional pain he's in and that he is not a hypochondriac.

When we fought the battle in our church (not the church I currently pastor) that I mentioned in the previous chapter, my reaction took me by surprise. I had been feeling pretty good because the church had been at peace for some time. I believed I had recovered from the devastation of betrayals by friends and loved ones, betrayals I had suffered in the first couple of years after we planted the church. What I had not expected was that a number of my family members (not my wife), most of whom were members of the church, abandoned me - or seemed to do so - in my hour of need. Some even led the opposition.

The abandonment lasted only about a week before most understood and took up my cause, but the damage had already been done. None of those inner physical resources I just mentioned were there for me to draw upon. It was as if a great black hole had opened up beneath me and was sucking me downward with a muddy swirling motion. I remember thinking what a relief it would be just to let go and be completely crazy. My mother-in-law, who lives with us and who has experienced two nervous breakdowns of her own, overheard Beth and me talking about my symptoms. She turned ashen-white and began to pray. She knew what was happening and feared for me. I took a vacation, demanding that I not be seen or contacted by anyone until I returned. Once gone, I was able to hold my own for a week or two, but then the depression worsened until I felt my world was coming to an end. In the midst of it all, one of our elders heard the call of the Spirit and he and his wife took Beth and me out to a movie and for coffee afterwards. It was the right moment. My grip on reality was restored as they spoke positive truth to me concerning the condition of our church and the effectiveness of my ministry. I began to recover.

The servant who has reached this stage of wounding suffers frighteningly distorted perceptions and almost uncontrollable paranoia. He finds himself afraid in relation to nearly every aspect of his ministry. Offerings will be inadequate; the church will lose members; longstanding and powerful leaders will leave; and on and on. Who will betray him next? Who is talking behind his back? From past experience he knows no one will stand with him and he begins to picture conflict situations in which he walks out or resigns. He mentally rehearses blistering speeches he wishes he could make in response to hurtful situations.

His inability to receive love worsens. He's so bruised that even the embrace of a safe family member causes pain. Emotional withdrawal is now nearly constant and moments of vulnerability are most rare. I took a long time even to learn to kiss my wife again. In the depth of my wounding I couldn't stand to have anything or anyone "in my face" demanding a response - and in my cognitively distorted state, that's what it felt like. The simple offer of frontal affection at first irritated me, and then ignited rage if my barriers weren't respected.

Ministry during this stage is enormously painful. I can recall counseling sessions in which I cried out to God in mortal desperation, "Please! Make it stop!!" as some troubled complainer droned on. The wounded one has nothing left to give. Every sermon, every teaching, every bit of counsel given requires gargantuan effort on his part.

Taking an extended vacation may help, but often only serves to make matters worse, as it did for me. In some cases, the wounded one may be so filled with anxiety concerning what might be going wrong in the ministry at home that limited doses of contact with work may be necessary to keep him in touch with reality.

Resistance to all sorts of addictive behavior becomes impaired at this stage. I worry that many burnout victims may be getting chemical help from their personal physicians at a time when dependency on drugs is a real danger. Drugs often only suppress the problem, rather than solve it, and so there will be a debt to pay later. In my personal opinion, medicines should be taken only when needed to bring just enough clarity to enable real therapeutic discussion to occur in counseling. They must never be seen as the solution. My personal physician and I agreed that even so innocent a drug as a sleeping pill would have been dangerous for me, so I resolved not to use them and sought answers in my faith.

I found myself retreating into video games. I was addicted to them, but they didn't relieve my stress. Anyone who has played them knows they're a very tense way to have fun. I know one burnout victim who became obsessed with television. Yet another became a rude and idolatrous fanatic for television football. There are as many choices as there are people.

Continually suppressed emotions come back in distorted form and the burnout victim has probably long been inadequately dealing with his feelings. I felt I had been *forced* to suppress mine. My upbringing programmed it, and my experience in the church reinforced and confirmed it. If I shared what I really felt with anyone other than my wife - or with the elders later on - the shock waves in the fellowship were more trouble than the relief was worth. Our society is so sick about authority that any leader who shares a weakness or a sin too openly, or in the wrong company, will certainly pay for it later. The spirit of our society is to search for faults in leadership and then use them to tear down and to weaken the leader's effectiveness. When we can't find a legitimate flaw, we just invent one and then convince ourselves it's true. The wolves among the flock use the leader's weakness as a pretext to attack and accuse, while the weak and insecure find in it an excuse to spread poison among others who are weak. If the leader can be made to appear smaller, they can feel bigger in their smallness, and so they welcome every opportunity to bring the leader down. All of it adds to the stress, and, as a result, the downward slide of the wounded burnout victim accelerates. I remember thinking bitterly that because of the ministry, I had neither the right nor the time to feel.

Under normal conditions, morality is a settled gift in a strong man of God. Temptations come, as they always do, but are routinely bested by the exercise of a sanctified will. In the deeply burned-out, however, key strengths have often been catastrophically eroded so that whatever cracks remain in his inner being, whatever areas of flesh or of sin that God has not been allowed to transform, may become gaping chasms under pressure. By means of natural strength and spiritual integrity he's controlled his sin nature in the past, but his capacity to control is now dangerously eroded or gone.

Therefore, the third-stage burnout victim may

find himself compulsively violating what he knows to be clear biblical moral imperatives. The following are confessions I've heard in counseling. He may be irresistibly drawn to pornography and be driven deeper into wounding by the stress produced by the guilt over his attraction. He may find himself compulsively masturbating as a way of relieving emotional pressures. He may begin to think unexplainably violent thoughts and to visualize himself doing violent things. He may find himself drawn to women other than his wife. He may begin to drink excessively in private. He may begin to drive too fast too much of the time. This list could go on and on. All of it adds to his guilt burden. He can't understand the loss of control that has led him to do, think and feel these things. Guilt over this loss of control produces more stress, which drives him even deeper into incapacity.

His confidence in his anointing and in his ability to minister may be utterly destroyed and he may even question his calling. This is largely due to a loss of perspective. In his weakened condition he can focus only on small things, rather than perceive the whole picture. Immediate problems seem eternal and insoluble, when, under normal conditions, he would be able to see them as temporary. It seems to him that his best efforts and most costly expenditures of energy have not produced the fruit he needs to sustain himself. He has given the best he has to offer and has received scorn and criticism in return. If he counsels, he may have forgotten that people take years to change, rather than days or months. He sees every setback suffered by a counselee as his personal failure. He may talk of leaving his ministry and may even hint at suicide. Take this threat seriously in most cases and do what you can to protect him from himself. Better to be wrong and safe than wrong and wishing you'd listened. Usually such talk is just catharsis, noise to be heard and ignored, but you can never be certain.

Ministry to Stage Three

Don't be a "Job's comforter". At this depth of devastation, avoid confronting the wounded one with the bitter-root judgments or sin that may have created his problem. At this stage he is in no condition at all to do that kind of introspection or to deal with the healing process associated with it. There are no resources left in him to do so. Often, he has already crucified himself with self-examination and has come up empty-handed. He's probably repented in every way he knows how and, like Job, he may know by now that the suffering under which he labors will not be alleviated by repentance for some hidden sin. But whether it is or is not the fruit of sin in his life, this is not the time for corrective ministry. "Nouthetic" (confrontive) counseling may serve only to drive him over the edge. Corrective ministry is possible only *after* some recovery of strength. Don't analyze the roots of the problem unless he asks for analysis, and then do so only sparingly.

In most cases, deliverance ministry is a foolish approach. Spirits of oppression are **not** the source of his problem. He will not get better as a result of your prayers for deliverance and will only feel more betrayed by God for the failure to improve. Spirits may be contributing to the problem, but they are not the root of it. If you must cast demons off of, or out of him, do so where he cannot hear.

It sounds strange, but it may cause more harm than good to tell the wounded one that God loves him. He can't believe that God loves him and is convinced that the evidence points to the absence of that love. Your affirmation of it only brings him face to face with his pain in that regard. Tell him that *you* love him. He may not believe it, but it's more tangible than the love of a God he can neither see nor any longer feel. It will then be your responsibility to prove that you mean what you say by not failing him or betraying him.

Don't tell the third stage sufferer what inner imperfections you believe or see that God is burning out of his nature, or that this is a sanctifying, purifying experience sent or used by God to "get the 'gunk' out". It may be true that God is, in fact, using the situation to accomplish just such a cleansing, but to the wounded one God is a betrayer and he has had enough of pain. Besides he already instinctively knows that what you're saying is true. If he didn't, he'd be long gone already.

Respect his fences and his withdrawal. Be secure enough not to take them as personal rejection. He simply can no longer respond normally to others and, if he is pushed to do so, the result may be an explosion of rage, followed by a deeper flight from relationships. Don't demand that he talk to you or that he listen to your advice. Let him choose the sharing times.

Don't talk to him about time management. This is seldom, if ever, the problem. Management of time is just another thing to do, something to work at, and he can't take any more of that. Don't tell him he needs to delegate more of his work. He's been let down too often by those who didn't follow through on their tasks and can no longer risk being wounded in that area. If you want to take some of the burden, just *do* it and tell him afterwards.

Don't tell him to praise God *for* all things (Ephesians 5:20). This is wonderful scriptural counsel to give a healthy sufferer, but it's a cruel burden to place on an incapacitated wounded servant. He *can't* do it. His best approach to God is an honest cry of rage. All I had left at this point was my honesty concerning how I felt. That's how I knew I still had a relationship with God. I called Him every name in the book, both fair and foul, and He was big enough not be offended by it as I got it off my chest. Better to have an angry relationship in which communication continues than to have no relationship at all.

As with stage two burnout, don't deliver face-to-face prophecies that *must* be responded to, no matter how encouraging their content may be. That's sandpaper on open wounds. Write it out and send it by mail or deliver it by hand with the understanding that it can be read later, privately.

The best praying for a stage three burnout

49

victim is done at a respectful distance. Don't tell your wounded one what you're praying for because that makes him feel responsible to do something about it. Just let him know you're praying and that you care and let it stop there. He'll be able to take encouragement from such assurance without feeling any pressure to respond.

Love him in ways that demand no response. Whether you are family or friend, don't "get in his face" with frontal hugs or penetrating eye contact. Many wounded ones absolutely cannot stand the intensity of full frontal interaction, so let hugs be sideways or from behind and don't demand eye contact. Let expressions of love take the form of a touch on the hand or an affectionate poke in the ribs.

Listen. Be available. The rare moment of vulnerability may surface at any time. I used to talk to Beth in bed, late at night, usually rousing her from a sound sleep. Under any other circumstances, that would be the height of insensitivity, but I couldn't help it. That's when I was able to spill my pain, and I knew that if I let the moment go, I'd not be able to manufacture it later. Beth understood more than anyone else that I didn't want answers to my sharing, that it was enough for me just to be able to express myself to one who wouldn't be dragged down by my gloomy outlook.

Believe in your sufferer, and tell him about it. Beth used to assure me over and over again that I was a good pastor and father, because I was no longer certain I was a good anything. See and affirm the wounded one's gifts and don't waver in your faith for him.

Send encouraging gifts and cards of love and appreciation for what the wounded one has given to you, but remember not to demand any sort of response.

At the appropriate time, pursue the wounded one and speak truth to him about what's right and good in the ministry and in his life. Time this carefully in the Spirit, because, if approached at the wrong time, the wounded one can be driven further into withdrawal. A good illustration is the story I told earlier about one of the elders who came to me at the bottom of my despair and spoke truth to me again. The third stage burnout victim is in danger of completely losing his grip on reality. While withdrawal is needed as a tool for healing, it can also be a perceptual prison in which there are no correctives against a fatal loss of perspective. Without those correctives, the nightmare of despair can become both bottomless and endless.

5
Personal Survival
WHAT THE WOUNDED ONE CAN DO

At the seminar on burnout the Elijah House team and I taught in Spokane, Washington all those years ago, someone asked how I survived my own experience. There were many facets to my answer. I have a wife who instinctively did for me what needed to be done. At a crucial point in my walk through that wilderness, a friend tracked me down and spoke the truth to me in a way I could hear and respond to. A few were quickened by the Lord to send me encouragement in the mail or to deliver written prophecies by hand that I could read later. But by and large, most people did all the wrong things. I come from parents who are at the top of the list of Christian counselors in this country, and *they* did all the wrong things!

Many of the items I discuss in this chapter are survival decisions and skills you will need should the Lord choose to take you further along the way and plunge you into the dark night of the soul. I regard my years of burnout as a time when God taught me much of what I needed to know in order to successfully find my way through the dark night of the soul before He plunged me into it. I was therefore able to go into that deeper wilderness having already made the most crucial decisions.

The most important thing that enabled me to survive was the *gift of mental discipline* bestowed on me by grace somewhere in the course of my life. Part of it was the training I received as a child when I was not allowed to act out my emotions in ways that might be destructive to others. That training formed a second-nature restraint that I could rely on without having to work at it very hard. I was given a good foundation in both affection and discipline so that, in the midst of the most severe tests, I have been able to know what I know well enough to survive.

I realize many of us weren't given this training as children. Without it, the battle for control is immeasurably more difficult, but still winnable. I know one young minister in the depths of wounding who lost control and became abusive with his wife and son for a time. The walls of restraint hadn't been provided in his early life and so he broke under the pressure of the crisis he faced. In his early ministry and then in the early stages of his wounding, the discipline of prayer and of his Christian walk kept him kind and gentle, but he was horrified at what came out of him later.

He exploded, becoming verbally and even physically abusive with his family, then fought for discipline with all his failing strength. He struggled. He wept. He despaired. He even considered divorcing his wife so that he would not abuse again. He pled for the Lord's discipline and sought wise and compassionate counsel. In the end, the Lord Himself provided for him the discipline he lacked and God became his Father. So - it's more difficult, but it's possible. The war *can* be won.

Even at the depth of my own wounding, I

disciplined myself to weigh the consequences of losing control against the pain of hanging on, and therefore refused to surrender to insanity. I knew that every time I acted on my anger, I would only create more stress for myself than I was already suffering. I knew most people could never understand and would only be hurt by my outbursts. Matters would be worse in the end. If I turned to accusation of others as a means of alleviating inner pressures, I would only drive people to defend themselves by attacking me.

I knew that if I couldn't make it work at Cornerstone, there was no place else for me to go. My integrity would forever be in question, even in my own eyes. Rather than quit, I stayed until I knew I had done what I was called to do.

I was also able to take into account what my children would lose if I fell apart. Because I knew that the pain I would suffer for taking their heritage from them would be worse than the pain I was already experiencing, I hung on. I chose to stand and I *made* myself do it. I *decided* to believe, no matter what. The first principle of survival is, therefore, to **know what you know for your own sake and for the sake of others who depend on you**. You won't always succeed, but the effort may enable you to survive.

During this time I learned that feelings simply exist. I mean that in and of themselves, feelings are morally neutral. As an extension of our sinful flesh, they are at least forgivable. There is a certain sense in which we are helpless to control those feelings that don't line up with God's nature, so that our only hope for victory is to confess our helplessness and receive the Lord's mercy. Feelings don't necessarily have substance, nor do they necessarily reflect reality. And they are profoundly poor determiners of what I should do in the real world. They have a function, but that function does not include making decisions for action. Their function in my inner life is analogous to that of the nervous system in my physical body. They are designed to tell me that something is wrong by sending a pain message, or that something feels good, but that's where it ends.

I therefore survived, in part, by learning to separate what I felt from what I did. I learned that *what is right to do, or true to believe, often has little or nothing to do with what I feel.* I can have a feeling in one part of myself and do the opposite of that feeling in another part of myself just because the doing of the thing is objectively right. Unfortunately, most of us stumble through life acting out our subjectivities, living as victims of our emotions and consistently reaping trouble for it.

The heart is more deceitful than all else And is desperately sick; who can understand it? Jeremiah 17:9

Living from a base in feelings is fine when feelings coincide with reality or with what is objectively right, but every one of us must somehow learn to do what is objectively right, even when our emotions conflict with what is objectively right. It seems to me this is the very definition of self control.

Know what you know, and insofar as your incapacity at the depth of your burnout will allow it, do what you know. You may not succeed. You may be too "wasted" in your own energies to succeed. But the effort may keep you sane, protect your loved ones and train into you an inner discipline that will yield huge dividends later.

The second principle of survival is to "embrace the fireball". I got the phrase from a dream a young college student once asked me to interpret. In the dream the Lord Jesus appeared to him and presented him with a ball of fire about the size of a basketball. He was instructed to hug it to himself. He obeyed and found the pain excruciating, but there was something terribly good about it, as well. I knew the Lord was about to plunge him into some kind of suffering intended to purify his heart, and that he was to embrace the "fire" rather than fight it.

> **Beloved, do not be surprised at the fiery ordeal among you, which comes upon you for your testing, as though some strange thing were happening to you; But to the degree that you share the sufferings of Christ, keep on rejoicing; so that also at the revelation of His glory, you may rejoice with exultation.** I Peter

4:12-13.

Therefore since Christ has suffered in the flesh, arm yourselves also with the same purpose, because he who has suffered in the flesh has ceased from sin,... I Peter 4:1.

Although I couldn't tolerate others telling me that my experience was for sanctification - it sounded like pious sermons from people who knew nothing - I knew within myself that it was. I even knew it was for no specific wrongdoing, at least not for a wrongdoing I could see at the time. In general, I have a task to perform for the Lord, a life calling, and for that task, my personality, gifts, abilities and even my way of meeting life must be honed, refined and changed.

There were times when I lost touch with this basic knowledge, times when the suffering just seemed senseless, but on the whole it contributed to my continuing sanity. I learned that the difference between redemptive suffering and destructive misery is the degree to which one fights, rather than accepts, the pain. I found a peculiar measure of peace in the embracing of it, even beneath the rage and frustration. I wasn't constant in that peace, but I did survive and I was certainly changed, although a great deal more change was to come through the dark night of the soul.

"Though He slay me, I will hope in Him" (Job

13:15). Job went on to protest his innocence and did, in fact, carry on a lengthy argument with God. But at the end, when the Lord revealed Himself, Job was compelled to admit:

> **I have heard of Thee by the hearing of the ear; But now my eye sees Thee; Therefore I retract, And I repent in dust and ashes.**
> Job 42:5-6.

Job did not and could not describe what it was he'd learned. I myself, even now, would have difficulty describing what's different about me and my relationship with God, but people who've known me through the years notice it. I'm better listened to than I was in the years before burnout and the dark night of the soul burned their imprint into me. I handle crises better. I'm simply a better leader and a more whole family man.

One of the most important lessons I've learned is that knowledge comes from study, but wisdom comes only through suffering. I have therefore determined to welcome suffering and have developed a new understanding of what the Preacher meant when he wrote:

> **Sorrow is better than laughter, For when a face is sad a heart may be happy. The mind of the wise is in the house of mourning, While the mind of fools is in the house**

of pleasure. Ecclesiastes 7:3-4.

Learn to love obedience for obedience's sake. I used to love to serve the Lord because I loved the fruit I saw in my ministry. It was fun to produce for Him. Part of the suffering was that God took away my ability to produce by sending me a gang of locusts to eat it all up. I had to learn to obey, whether I saw fruit or not. It can be a dark walk, but I had to come to a point where it was enough for me emotionally just to know that I had done what God had asked me to do. I began to teach others that obedience to the Lord must be its own reward. The doing of ministry, and not the fruit of doing ministry, must ever be my joy.

Find a safe environment in which regularly to dump what you feel, and do the dumping as an act of obedience to God. It may not be easy, but it is certainly necessary. James 5:16 is much neglected among protestants today and especially among clergy, "Therefore, confess your sins to one another, and pray for one another, so that you may be healed."

In the burnout years at the church in Idaho my dumping place was our elders' group that met weekly as a fellowship with our wives. These men and women were partners with me in ministry and we had developed a trust relationship in spite of the many ways in which we failed one another. For a time, I made it a discipline to report to them weekly on my emotional state. They needed to know, and I needed to objectify what I felt by sharing it. There were times when I wanted to hide, but I worked against the impulse because I knew it spelled the difference between recovery and failure.

Learn not to share with wounders. A surprising number of well-intentioned church people are eager to show deepest concern and love for you and your condition, but not all are safe. These people appear in many forms and may be of either gender. "I would never hurt you," they promise, "Please tell me if I ever do." Don't you believe it!

I'll tell you my own story and you can adapt it to your situation. It's actually a composite of many stories, rather than just one, since there are people I'd like to protect.

Most, but not all, of the wounders that have crossed my path have been seriously broken people with a need to gain some kind of control over authority figures in their lives. Obviously this kind of problem can involve both men and women, but women seem more susceptible to the kind of thing I'm addressing. I realize I may take some abuse for a statement like that in this increasingly feminist society, but in my experience, this was true. This sort of woman "gentles" her way into the life of a male leader in emotional trouble until, in some weak moment when he's off-guard and feeling leaky, she gets him to spill a portion of his pain.

Because these women tend to congregate with other women who share similar backgrounds of childhood abuse, it isn't long before a whole group of them are discussing this grave "concern" among themselves and praying up a storm, fanning the flames of their emotions and becoming more and more deluded. They don't believe they're speaking in any unrighteous way because, after all, these women with whom they share are their friends and they are just submitting their burdens and perceptions to trusted others for confirmation and balance. They may share these burdens with their husbands, as well, so that, if the man isn't exceptionally strong, he may be drawn into the talk and the delusion with her.

Before long, the group arrives at a solution for, or an analysis of, the leader's problem and they want to minister to it. The solution, and/or analysis, is usually way off the mark and often comes as a set of what sound like accusations, spoken, "in love," but which cut the wounded one to the heart. Then, when he rejects their "prophetic word" because of its inaccuracy, he is seen as one who doesn't listen and cannot receive correction. This sets off a round of new criticism and more talk.

Understand that these are well-intentioned saints of the Lord, acting with no awareness of what they're really doing. Love them, but avoid sharing with them anything of substance from your own heart.

I know of no better way to identify wounders and to avoid falling into their traps than to *listen to the Distant Early Warning System*. God has put into our mates, whether man or woman. They have a failsafe sense of when something or some individual poses a threat to us. It's there for our defense and we do well to heed it. Beth is an emotionally whole and balanced woman who has unfailingly spotted such hidden reefs and warned me ahead of time. I had to learn the hard way that she was right by suffering the situation I described above on an occasion or two. Today I listen.

If you're a third stage burnout victim, and you're not married, or if your spouse is wounded herself (or himself), then seek out reliable prophets in your flock who can warn you concerning impending doom and who can see the sin in the hearts of people. Then heed them for your own sake and for the sake of the fellowship you lead.

Feed your weakened spirit in ways that don't require energy expenditures. First, cleanse your mind of standard Christian pietistic ideas of how to get refreshment from the Lord, and then prepare yourself for something that may be different for you. Standard Christian piety is fine under normal conditions, but it often represents demands that can no longer be met by many deeply wounded ones. In His grace, God can refresh, instruct and correct His servants from a multitude of unlikely sources. Remember that He spoke to Balaam by the mouth of an ass. Sometimes we need to be surprised, even ambushed, by God when the old and familiar has lost its lustre. After such an ambush, the old and familiar takes on new life and is infused with a new ability to give refreshment.

Try listening to good music, both secular and sacred. At one point in the process of my recovery I got out some old Joni Mitchell records from my "hippie" days. Her poetry was marvelous and her music deeply melancholy, with an ever present reminder of a simpler life. Sometimes she sang in such a beautiful way of such dismal hopelessness that if the music weren't so good, the listener would be crushed. I was locked up emotionally and her music expressed something of what was inside of me. By expressing it, the music connected with what I felt and released what was so imprisoned. On numerous occasions I sat before the stereo and wept.

I went to movies like the *Rocky* series in which a nobody from a Philadelphia slum fought his way to the top of the world of boxing, was beaten and then fought his way back again. Along the way, he was restored to himself, learned to pray and became a family man. I own all five of that set on video. The *Star Trek* and *Star Wars* series both got to me. Both of those series are also in my video library. Both series were about people who snatched victory from the jaws of defeat, who came from behind to overcome powerful enemies, often with supernatural help. It didn't matter to me that the god of *Star Wars* is not the God of the Bible. The point was that all those little people overcame enormous opposition with the help of their god as they understood him - or "it" as "the Force" would be more properly referred to.

I reread J.R.R. Tolkien's *The Lord of the Rings* and a whole group of other fantasies by both Christian and non-Christian authors. I needed a fresh injection of imagination and magic (in its good and figurative sense) in my life in order to renew my sense of the supernatural. God gave that renewal to me in some of the world's great literature.

All of these books and movies were important to me because the theme common to all of them is recovery of power after a crushing defeat by an enemy who seems overwhelming and invincible. They tell of little men doing great things in the face of terrible odds. They include lessons on the misuse of power and on the strength to be found in weakness. They reminded me that I'm a winner by nature and by anointing and that I had a great God on my side. I hadn't lost the war, but the cost of fighting had left me so weakened and broken that I had forgotten what strength felt like.

These simple movies and wonderful books rekindled a dying flame and sent me soaring. God met me there. I'm not bothered at all that many of them are not Christian in their worldview. We don't need to be afraid of that sort of thing. Like most of us who would be reading this book, I had a lifetime of commitment to the Lord's Word with me to automatically filter truth from pollution. God lifted out of their pagan settings the valuable insights that I needed to hear and made them shine for me.

To date, I've read Tolkien five times and have seen each of the *Rocky* movies, and each of the space movies, more times than I care to admit. More recently I've drawn inspiration from the movie *Braveheart* which I have seen six times. Some of you may think me seriously deluded for all of this, but I said at the beginning that I didn't write this book to start a debate. Think what you like, I know what I know. God used those secular sources to revitalize the reading of His Word for me and, as a result, I saw things in the Scriptures I hadn't seen before. The Bible had new encouragement in it as God refreshed me from some unlikely springs. Watch Luke Skywalker battle the evil Darth Vader, or Rocky defeat the powerful Russian who had killed his friend in the ring, then open your Bible and read of David as he faced Goliath or of Moses standing before great Pharaoh and you will know what I mean.

Others might find useful inspiration in the heroic stories of King Arthur or Robin Hood. Still others might be drawn to some works of great classical music or to poetry. Time spent in the vastness of nature might recall greatness and rekindle imagination concerning the wonder and power of God. Jesus Himself frequently went to the mountaintop to pray.

In short, nourish your spirit on great music, great poetry, heroic stories and films, or whatever else rekindles your dying flame. And don't limit the kinds of vehicles God can use to do that. All true beauty and truth come from Him. Whatever you consume, let it stand under the judgment of the eternal Word, the Bible. All good wine must be cleansed by passing through that True Filter.

Get someone to lie for you. Really! Stay with me, now! What I mean is that you need to establish some protection for yourself that you are not personally responsible to maintain. My wife and my secretary do this for me today at New Song Fellowship, the church I pastor in Denver. When they see that my energies are expended, they sweetly and very professionally keep people away, often without checking with me. They know I say yes when I shouldn't.

In the burnout years back at Cornerstone, my wife and my mother-in-law (who still lives with us) took care of that boundary. The church phone rang both at the church facility and at our home and I determined never to answer it myself. Here's the "lying" part! My wife is clever enough to tell selective truths about my availability. She tells you only what you really must know so that you hang up the phone understanding that I cannot be reached, but not feeling blown off. My mother-in-law, on the other hand, doesn't think as quickly as my wife does, and was therefore prone to tell you I wasn't at home, when, in fact, I was. A sanctified lie.

The point is that there are times when I'm not the one to decide when I've spent too much of myself. I'm not good at saying no to people. I've become better at it through the years, but it's a long way from "better" to "good".

Still worried about that "lying" part? In Joshua 2, Rahab the harlot lied to the defenders of Jericho in order to protect the spies sent from Joshua to spy out the city. In Judges 4, Jael deceived Sisera in order to kill him for the sake of the people of Israel. Both women were praised for their acts and stand today as heroines of the faith. 'Nuff said? Make a place, albeit a small and cautious one, for sanctified lying when you need to protect your energies and there seems to be no other way. And let someone else do it.

   Don't automatically assume that the cause of your burnout must be some personal sin or character flaw. It may very well be, but at the depth of your wounding, that search may not be helpful. Job suffered terribly, but not as a result of any of the usual personal shortcomings we might expect or look for. Although his suffering was not the result of clear unrighteousness on his part, he was changed by the experience, and his personal relationship with God was transformed. More on this in a later chapter. For now, suffice it to say that the same transformation will be yours if you but wait it out.

   When you can't praise God, be honest. Pour out your pain. Even call Him names. He'll probably fall off His throne laughing. Suppression of emotion brings a terrible reaping, while open honesty cleanses. In my deepest rage and despair I even swore at Him. I discovered He doesn't have virgin ears and that His presence is the one completely safe place in all the world in which I can be whatever I happen to be at the moment. It isn't as if He doesn't already know what's in my heart anyway! Better to hurl my honest rage and accusation at God than not to pray at all. You won't have to read far in the Psalms to find that there is more than ample scriptural precedent for expressing oneself before God in this way.

   If the obstacles you face in your situation seem too overwhelming to beat, at least don't quit. The fact that you don't quit will itself win the day for you. Ephesians 6:10ff., the great spiritual warfare passage, places its strongest emphasis on, "standing firm." You aren't required to conquer or take land or personally defeat the spiritual hosts of wickedness. It isn't even necessary that you be able to function at full capacity in your standing firm. You have only to refuse to move for the victory to be assured.

First, by your refusal to move, you give God room to work the sort of transformation in your heart that He made in Job's heart. Often those who flee the scene of suffering only remove themselves from the fire God set to test them, and they cheat themselves of the strength and wisdom that develop only in the heat of tribulation and death.

Second, in your standing firm you break the heart of your enemy, whether that enemy is a spiritual force, a situation or a person. I once told a troublemaker, "I'm tougher than anyone here and I'll be here long after you're gone." Her whole crowd was soon history while I reaped years of abundance after that. And your adversary, the Devil, is in an even worse position than your human opponent. You have eternity in which to stand. He doesn't. His doom is appointed, his time limited. You may be so broken that you can no longer fight, but you can at least refuse to get out of the ring.

Know your innocence. Often your burnout is the result of a barrage of accusations from those to whom you minister and for whom you've poured forth your best gifts of love. Because you know you've made mistakes, your tendency may be to try to wear what they are saying about you. Somehow you feel that if you could just do everything right, everyone would love you for it, and because they're not loving you, it must be your fault.

This is, of course, a foolish assumption. There comes a time when you must call a halt to self-examination and introspection and take stock of your integrity. Claim your innocence. There came a time when I finally had to say, "I have not done that of which you accuse me! I have not manipulated. I never said what you accuse me of having said. I didn't mean what you insist I meant when I said thus-and-such. I did not betray to others what you shared in confidence; it was you, yourself, who leaked the information and it was those trusted friends you leaked it to who passed it around."

I think you get the idea. I wasn't perfect, but I had not sinned against those people - at least not in the ways they thought I had. I had to be driven to the point of rage before I could take this stand. I had nearly destroyed myself with misplaced guilt, doubts and questions by the time I got to that point, but it was a tremendous relief when I did

Those of us with pastor's hearts have a very difficult time accepting the fact that people are basically nasty. We want to believe in them, and we'd rather blame ourselves than face the possibility that the heart of a loved one might be as black as night and set on destruction.

Get mad. Pray the "bloody" psalms. God will know what to do with them, even if, in your rage, you intend more than is righteous. Do this, not to wish evil on your enemies, but as a kind of catharsis before God. Get the hurt out of your system. Pour it out to God by means of the words of Scripture. In this praying you will find a holy kind of release, while spiritual power is released to defeat your enemies. I would qualify this by saying that what was alright during my burnout years was not acceptable later in the dark night of the soul. In the dark night of the soul, God dealt with my anger and held me, as he still does, to a strict regime of praying genuine blessing on my enemies. Jesus said, **Love your enemies**, but during the burnout years, it helped to pray these disturbingly violent psalms. Here are some quotes:

> **Contend, O Lord, with those who contend with me; Fight against those who fight against me. Take hold of buckler and shield, And rise up for my help. Draw also the battle-ax to meet those who pursue me; ...Let those be ashamed and dishonored who seek my life; Let those be turned back and humiliated who devise evil against me... Let destruction come upon him unawares; And let the net which he hid catch himself; Into that very destruction let him fall.** Psalm 35:1-8.

> **O God, shatter their teeth in their**

mouth; Break out the fangs of the young lions, O Lord. Let them flow away like water that runs off; When he aims his arrows, let them be as headless shafts. Psalm 58:6-7.

Save me, O God, For the waters have come up to my soul. I have sunk in deep mire, and there is no foothold; I have come into deep waters, and the flood overflows me. I am weary with my crying; my throat is parched; My eyes fail while I wait for my God. Those who hate me without cause are more than the hairs of my head; Those who would destroy me are powerful. What I did not steal, I then have to restore... For Thy sake I have borne reproach; Dishonor has covered my face. I have become estranged from my brothers, And an alien to my mother's sons... Reproach has broken my heart, and I am so sick. And I looked for sympathy, but there was none, And for comforters, but I found none. They also gave me gall for my food, And for my thirst they gave me vinegar to drink. May their table before them become a snare;

And when they are at peace, may it become a trap. May their eyes grow dim so that they cannot see, And may their loins shake continually. Pour out Thine indignation on them, And may Thy burning anger overtake them. May their camp be desolate; May none dwell in their tents... May they be blotted out of the book of life, And may they not be recorded with the righteous. Psalm 69.

O God of my praise, Do not be silent! For they have opened the wicked and deceitful mouth against me; They have spoken against me with a lying tongue. they have also surrounded me with words of hatred, And fought against me without cause. In return for my love they act as my accusers; But I am in prayer. Thus they have repaid me evil for good, And hatred for my love. Appoint a wicked man over him; And let an accuser stand at his right hand. When he is judged, let him come forth guilty; And let his prayer become sin. Let his days be few; Let another take his office. Let

his children wander about and beg; And let them seek sustenance far from their ruined homes. Let the creditor seize all that he has; And let the stranger plunder the product of his labor. Let there be none to extend lovingkindness to him, Nor any to be gracious to his fatherless children. Let his posterity be cut off; In a following generation let their name be blotted out. Psalm 109:1-13.

In the end, each of those who falsely accused and persecuted me during the burnout years was shamed before the congregation. While I did next to nothing, God sovereignly revealed their sin before the whole flock until with one voice the fellowship cried, "Enough!"

When the judgment of God falls on such people, it is redemptive, but when they reap the Law, full-grown, the end is devastation. The judgment of God restores the repentant heart while the reaping of the Law simply destroys. "God is not mocked; for whatever a man sows, this he will also reap" (Galatians 6:7). Therefore, in the mystery of God, I believe such bloody prayers are really prayers for mercy, prayer that it will be the judgment of God and not the reaping of the Law that comes to these people.

The tragedy in our case was that most of those who did these things to me were never able to repent.

As I followed their histories after they left us, I discovered a consistent pattern of disaster. There were bankruptcies, incest, family break-ups and house fires, to name but a few. It is a fearsome thing to fall into the hands of the living God!

Yet, if any one of these people ever came to my door needing help, I'd give it. One or two of them wouldn't be allowed back into any flock I pastored without some real repentance and change, but all would be welcome to my personal ministry.

6
BREAKING DESTRUCTIVE LIFE PATTERNS

Burnout victims are often captives to what they do, sacrificing self and health well beyond the true call of God. I remember thinking - and rightly so - that my life and faith should be a model for others. Late in the burnout years, the next thought became, "But where is my joy? Would I invite others into this pain I'm in? Is the Christian walk an invitation to fatigue? Do I really want others to be as unbalanced as I am? Why would anyone, looking at the quality of my life, want to join me in it?" Because of the questions, recovery from burnout and the rediscovery of joy became issues of personal integrity. How could I preach the peace of God when I had so little of it myself?

Unhealthy life patterns needed breaking. In describing them, I've tried not to duplicate things already covered in previous chapters except where emphasis is needed.

The Personal Obligation Pattern

Most burnout victims in ministry feel personally obligated to everyone. Sometimes the problem is a fear of not being liked or loved for saying no once in a while. Or the victim may genuinely feel that, without his direct involvement, terrible things will happen in the lives of those who look to him for ministry. He has an overblown sense of his own responsibility and too little faith in Jesus to take care of situations. He may see the failures of others as his own and therefore can't risk letting others fail. The point is that he can't withdraw from perceived obligations often enough or long enough to remain healthy. He is so locked into this sense of personal responsibility for things, and is so imprisoned by his inability to say no, that he won't even permit others to say no on his behalf.

I began to learn to say no by becoming so angry with the escalating demands of the sick people in the church I pastored, and by becoming so frustrated with my own condition, that discomfort drove me to take action. I'm still not good at it, even after all these years, but I try. For instance, the telephone rings and it's Melvin calling again with the same story he tells again and again, with the same pain, again and again and again. I'm not home, but my wife promises I'll return his call. I don't. Angrily I don't. Feels good, too. And Melvin survives. Amazing!

The building committee is meeting on my day off. They'll make decisions concerning the shape of our new building that I'll hate later. My pastoral perspective is needed. The chairman knew better than to schedule the meeting for that day, darn his hide! Well, I'm not going! Take that! Talked to the architect two days later. Corrected some errors. Everybody lived.

Planning our vacation. Gosh, I need it this year! But we're supposed to be with family. Aunt Maimie will be there. She's been judging me for fifteen years and she'll be at it again. She won't say anything to me directly, but I'll feel it in the air and her husband will hear about it later. Can't handle that this year. I need this vacation away from the stress of constantly juggling other people's feelings and I won't get it with her there. I refuse to deal with that situation again this year! The family will be upset if we don't come? Good! I won't be there to see it! Now where's another place we can go to be alone?

The Self-Sacrifice Pattern

My family has an inherited disease. My minister father has it. My brothers and sisters have it. I have it. It's an attitude that goes something like this: "If I'm not working to exhaustion, I'm not working hard enough." Fun is a waste of precious ministry time. Therefore, time for fun means time for guilt. Exercise is time taken away from work time. More guilt. Then guilt for not exercising. Even sleep is a distraction from the task of ministry. Hobbies are out. They're for the uncommitted who have time for such empty pursuits. The answer to this one is so obvious I shouldn't even have to spell it out.

Here are some solutions I found for myself. When we still lived in Idaho while I pastored Cornerstone, Beth and I bought a week at a timeshare condominium. We couldn't afford it, but we knew we needed something like it. For that week each year, we left our kids with their grandmother while the two of us spent a week alone together in shameless self-indulgence. And God approved so heartily that He enabled us to pay for it! I don't know what it will take for you, but find some way to cultivate a little "holy selfishness". Indulge yourself!

Concerning the issue of *my* time, God spoke to me directly on two occasions. One afternoon in the depth of my burnout when I was too tired to work (but hadn't the courage to leave the office and actually *look* like I wasn't working) God said simply, "Instead of feeling guilty for these stolen moments, why not thank Me for this opportunity to rest?" Obediently, I began a simple but refreshing discipline of doing just that for a few moments each day. Try it. You'll like it. You'll feel like a kid with his hand in the forbidden cookie jar for a while, but you'll like it just the same and it may help save your sanity.

There is, of course, the simple principle that, "All work and no play makes Jack a dull boy." Play time is holy time. I used to feel guilty for taking time out with the one I mentioned earlier who would come over to my house and jokingly ask my wife if I could come out and play. A good laugh serves at least as well as twenty minutes in prayer for the release of tension and the refreshment of the soul. **A joyful heart is a good medicine, But a broken spirit dries up the bones** (Proverbs 17:22). Take time for some things you enjoy, and reject the guilt.

The second time He spoke on this issue He said, "If you don't start exercising, you're going to die." I knew I wasn't in imminent danger of losing my life, but I was in serious danger of losing something important to my life that I wouldn't have been able to recover. Perhaps it's an echo of my Osage Indian heritage on my father's side, but my personal makeup is such that strength is important to me - both physical and spiritual. Strength has been one of God's best natural gifts to me. I know, too, that ever since God formed man from dust and breathed his personal spirit into him, body and spirit have been interdependent. Physical health profoundly affects spiritual health, and vice versa. I was becoming desperately weak and sick in my body because of the stress in my life, and it was affecting me spiritually as well.

So deeply burned out and emotionally wounded was I that I couldn't find the strength to begin an exercise program on my own initiative, despite the Lord's warning. But I've learned that when I'm unable to obey the Lord freely, He'll set up a situation in which I'm compelled to do so. Not that He violates my free will. It's just that I gave Him blanket permission long ago to do with me as He would, and I've not yet withdrawn it. My father (the earthly one) began to notice the deterioration in my health and purchased a membership for me at a local athletic club. Because he had spent money, my personal obligation pattern clicked in - beneficially for once - and I began to exercise. I chose body-building because that's what I enjoy. For you, it might be racquet ball or jogging or swimming. The point is that exercise is crucial to the recovery process for any burnout victim.

That was eleven years ago and I still work out regularly, although I've dropped body building in favor of forms of exercise that keeps me skiing in a healthy way. I started body building with the same fervor I would have invested in anything I attempted and eventually burned out on the intensity, but not before I topped out with twenty-eight inch thighs, eighteen inch biceps and a forty-eight inch chest. For a pastor, an intimidating physique isn't necessarily an asset so I backed off long before I changed my form of exercise! In the beginning, however, I felt guilty for spending so much time on something not related to ministry, but the gym or the ski slopes are still places where I don't have to talk "church" unless I choose to. In the gym or on the ski lift, I'm just another human being, not a ministry machine/superman. If I want to pray, I can do so even while grunting out that last repetition on the leg press machine or fearing for my life in the middle of a huge jump off a high cornice.

Furthermore, my time in the gym - or on the mountain - is one of the few contacts I have with the world outside the church that doesn't involve work on behalf of the church. Exercise is both physically satisfying and tangibly rewarding, while most of the rest of my daily routine is mental and emotional and not immediately rewarding. Such contact helps keep me out of the "Christian ghetto" and in touch with real people "out there". From time to time I do get an opportunity to share the gospel with some curious or hungry soul fascinated by the rare spectacle of pastor with muscle - or a 46 year old who skiis like a kid - but that's not why I go.

Please understand, I'm not a physician, so accept or reject what I am about to say, depending on whether I make sense to you. My body knows - and my chiropractor confirms - that stress produces toxins which the body has a way of storing in its tissues when it can't filter them out fast enough. Over a period of time these can damage the digestive system, weaken muscles and ligaments and alter body chemistry in ways that affect moods and mental processes, among other things. Stress is particularly hard on the heart and the adrenal gland. Exercise helps eliminate those stored toxins and aids in restoring healthy body chemistry. It strengthens the heart muscle, helps the adrenal gland begin secreting adrenalin normally again and restores weakened connective tissues, tendons and ligaments. All of this contributes to reduction and elimination of the physical pain and chronic illness so many burnout victims experience and that their doctors have such a problem diagnosing. It also helps reestablish an overall sense of wellbeing and helps renew the body's ability to withstand emotional stress and physical diseases.

The procedure I recommend is that you see your personal physician for a complete physical exam in order to determine what level of exercise you can safely undertake and at what levels of intensity. Since you have depleted your nutritional reserves, consider asking him to refer you to a qualified nutritionist who can help you rebuild those reserves. At a minimum, you should clean up your dietary habits. Most of us, in this day and age, have some good awareness of what food is healthy and what is not. So just do it!

After your check-up, go to an athletic club or gym where good instruction is given. If options are available, shop around and ask questions until you find which club has the best instructors. Tell your instructor about the results of your physical exam, explain whatever personal goals you have for exercising and let the professional design an enjoyable program appropriate and effective for you. Or go shopping for those in-line skates or running shoes. The point is to get at it!

For the first month or more, you may feel a bit ill both during and after your workouts. Unaccustomed to exertion, you may experience headaches as a result of your workouts. Each of your early workouts will be a burden and you'll want to quit. Some days you'll feel you're just too tired to go. Ignore all of this. Your body is cleansing itself and your cells are releasing those stored toxins into the bloodstream where your natural filters can eliminate them. Stick with it faithfully and you'll find yourself a confirmed "sweathog", addicted to the satisfying, full sensation of fatigued muscles. You'll look better and you'll feel better in every way. You'll notice your energy returning.

Don't con yourself into thinking you're too far gone or too tired to do this. Exercise is too important to your recovery for you to permit this kind of self-deception. There will be no full and permanent recovery without exercise. It's part of the healthy balance of body and spirit that God intended us to cultivate.

The Isolation Pattern

What I have to say concerning this pattern may threaten some cherished theologies concerning church life, but I'm not a bit sorry for it. Most of this section is specifically aimed at pastors, but much of it applies to lay leaders as well.

Most patterns of government practiced in the modern church are set up to keep the pastor isolated and to deprive him of having any real power to lead. None of us consciously desires that result, but that's often the effect. Most churches today are still governed as democracies in which the task of those who occupy offices of leadership is to carry out the will of the people as expressed in the vote of the majority or through a popularly elected board. This works well in secular government, but not in God's house. God's church was never designed to be a democracy carrying out the will of the people. It was formed as a *theo*cracy, ruled by God through His anointed and appointed servants who discern and carry out His will - and who have both freedom and authority to do so. Moses was not an elected official. Neither was Peter. Nor Paul. They were *leaders* appointed by God with authority to set direction. Each of them maintained a team for balance and for counsel, but the crucial element is that their teams were *their* teams, not groups of people thrust upon them by some democratic process of selection.

Because most churches function as democracies, rather than theocracies, elders (or their equivalents) - whom God intended to be the pastor's team in ministry - are elected by the people rather than appointed by authority as the Scriptures dictate.

In case after case, therefore, they fail to function as the pastor's team in ministry. In fact, they are often elected to their positions by factions opposed to the pastor, in order to place dissenting voices in high places. My father pastored a series of Congregational churches as I grew up and I watched this happen again and again. The results can be devastating, both to the church and to the pastor, as he is effectively crippled in his ability to carry out the vision God has given him for the church.

Because we operate our churches on non-biblical bases, we are burning our shepherds out. The pastor today usually stands alone, rather than in the midst of a trusted team with whom the ministry is genuinely shared. Everywhere I go I hear ministers speaking of this isolation, and looking for ways to break out of it. The suggested solution is usually to seek fellowship among fellow clergy from other flocks, but I find this terribly inadequate. There just isn't time enough for the kind of sharing and uplifting needed for this to be effective. Further, I know that for my own primary support system to be effective, it has to be with me in the daily crush of ministry. Although I need fellowship with other clergy outside my own church in order to keep a certain perspective, I have a greater need for people who live in my own situation to stand alongside me, people who carry the same burden.

I rarely feel the isolation anymore, as I did in the days when Cornerstone functioned under a version of democracy rather than theocracy. In those days, no matter what crisis we faced I'd find myself alone. The elected board seemed paralyzed and unable to learn to minister effectively with me and had little or no ability to stand firm under fire for the sake of the flock. Everybody suffered for it and the church was weakened.

Today, at New Song Fellowship, I have a full time and part time staff that I regard as our elders. They are my team. Together we lead the church in spiritual matters, as God has called us to. Our Administrative Board works with me and with our executive pastor on matters financial and contractual, but my staff team leads as they are called and anointed to do in all other matters. We share the burden together, cultivate vulnerability together and face the crises together. Since planting this church I have yet to experience any form of professional isolation.

I'm saying that unbiblical forms of church government are often a major cause of burnout among ministry professionals. It isn't the purpose of this book to tell you how to change the specific system under which you work, if that system is out of alignment with God's word. Every situation is unique and the Scripture leaves a lot of latitude for how a system of government can be set up theocratically. I can only say that under any system, the pastor or anointed lay leader must seek out those called to be close to and safe for him. Gather a team of trustworthy folk around you and utilize their gifts, both in ministry to the flock and for your own support. Ask God to reveal these people to you and then purposefully draw them to yourself. If you're too far gone to do this, then simply ask God Himself to sovereignly bring them into your life.

Some of you have been so badly burned and betrayed by trusted confidants and team members that this may seem too difficult - too much risk. It seemed this way to me at one time because I, too, had been deeply scarred by people I loved. The truth was that I had chosen the wrong people, and had yet to learn how to identify the faithful and true. But even through the bad choices I learned wisdom and so I continued to work at chosing people to walk with me. But no matter how good I have become at choosing a team, I must remember that even Jesus chose a Judas.

The Self-Abuse Pattern

This pattern is often rooted in a subconscious death wish. Life is a burden and you'd really like to die, so you poison yourself with practices certain to further destroy your already deteriorating body. The process may be subconscious, or you may have enough awareness to recognize the morbid pleasure you take in it. In either case, it must be stopped.

This pattern most often manifests in habits of diet and rest. Your eating habits have probably been atrocious, marked by irregular meal times and junk food eaten on the run. Even good meals are eaten too hurriedly. You overeat. You undereat. Certain food addictions or allergies may appear. As I indicated earlier in this book, you should consult a qualified nutritionist and begin to rebuild depleted reserves. Determine to eat regularly. Purposefully eat whole grains and other natural, unprocessed foods. No mystery here. Just good sense. And while you're doing it, remember you're fighting for your life and for the glory of God in you.

Rest is really the big issue. Most pastors and lay leaders regularly violate the Sabbath rest. God designed us to function best when we take one day in seven to stop, worship God and do what we ourselves enjoy. That's the law. There is a price to pay for violating that law that's not so much the wrath of God as it is simply the way reality works. If you're a leader, don't expect to accomplish a Sabbath rest on Sunday since that's the biggest workday of the entire week. Choose another day and leave the phone off the hook. Even my church leaders know not to call me with church business on my day off.

Most of us wounded ones are workaholics with an average work week running sixty hours at minimum. And we love it so! What noble martyrs we are! For the layperson fully dedicated to ministry, this translates into forty hours at a secular job and twenty or more for the church, all of which takes a toll on the body and the spirit. I frequently find myself racing from one set of demands to another at breakneck speed, leaving little or no room for rest between tasks, much less the kind of meditation in prayer that renews the soul and energizes ministry. Often I'm at my best level of performance when I'm running that way, and I'm loving every minute of it.

The problem is that I'm a lot like the car that rounds a corner at a hundred miles per hour, only to plow into the wall the driver didn't see coming. Suddenly, the resources are gone and I find myself emotionally, intellectually, creatively and physically empty. It's a difficult condition from which to recover. If I can't learn to see the wall coming, then at least I must learn to anticipate where and when it will most likely appear and slow down *before* I crash. That means establishing more reasonable patterns of rest and relaxation, even when I don't feel like I'm tired yet. I need to rest *before* I tire, because one inch from the wall often feels no different than ten miles.

By way of breaking the pattern, learn to do simple things like determining not to be the last one to leave the church on Sunday each week. Somehow I must find a way to beat that line of people who feel they absolutely must have five minutes of my time on the way out the door in which to pour out the woes of a lifetime - while hundreds of others clamor for my attention - and get answers worth hours of personal counseling. These days I try to give more weight to those little after church family obligations that arise from time to time, so that I can make legitimate excuses to get away by a reasonable hour.

A more effective thing I've done is to give the making of my schedule over to my wife and my secretary who do a better job than I of telling people I don't have a spot open for three weeks. I feel obligated to make room for them at whatever personal price. They don't. The whole process creates those little windows of rest in a busy schedule that can spell the difference between sanity and insanity.

The Prayer Pattern

Your prayer discipline probably has failed to refresh you for quite some time, if it hasn't evaporated altogether, and if you take a close look you'll probably find it needed revamping anyway. Most of us have been fed a diet of pietistic legalism about spending an hour a day alone with God. Don't get me wrong. That's still my goal, but times of burnout signal the need for change. Change often requires a dismantling of the old before the new can come.

Perhaps you've been taught a certain method for praying. Certain styles of language must be used. You begin with , "Dear God," and end with, "In Jesus' name," religiously, like a formula of address. In my childhood family I learned to listen to God during my daily devotional, to be silent before Him to hear His voice or to receive Scripture references to look up. I still do this, and I write in a notebook what I hear.

But during burnout it all became an empty ritual. I felt lost without my notebook, as if I couldn't pray without all the elements of the ritual present. Under normal circumstances, for healthy people, all that method is good stuff, but the deeply burned out servant of God often needs a radical change.

As my prayer discipline began to falter, I at first felt really guilty for spending so little time "on my knees" and I'd strive with all my failing strength to put it back together again. Inevitably I'd fail and then be driven further down by guilt. At last I heard the Lord Himself order me to stop it. The old pattern, steeped in all those legalisms and methods, just wouldn't work anymore. God wanted to do larger things through me. For that I needed a renewed means of communing with God.

In the midst of my despair over the absence of refreshment in my quiet time, and for my inability even to maintain the discipline of having one, God said, "I'll not speak to you as to other men."

"How then?" I pled in my confusion.

"Trust your instincts," came the reply.

I pondered that until I understood that the Lord was trying to rebuild my shattered confidence and teach me to trust in what He'd been so carefully building into me through brokenness. But I also realized with a start that nowhere does the Word of God mandate anything concerning daily devotions other than: 1) to "pray without ceasing" (I Thessalonians 5:17), and 2) to take in some piece of God's Word daily for the heart to meditate on continually (Psalm 119 and others). Good news! That leaves lots of room for creativity and change.

The Lord began to train into me a new awareness of how to pray without ceasing and to meditate on His Word. Rather than block out time in which to expend energy and force a concentration I could no longer generate, I could simply plant some portion of the Word in my mind and heart and let it resonate there all day long. I found that whatever I put into my heart, I meditated on subconsciously.

Insights would later float up out of nowhere, as if the computer had been running a background program and finally spit out the solution. My very instincts could be infused with the Word, and I could be more responsive to the need of the moment than I had been previously.

Even when I was healthier, one of my needs had been to steep the entire day more deeply in prayer, rather than relegate it exclusively to my daily devotional hour. I began to pray more in tongues than in English. For that period of time in my life, the energy expenditure was lower and the return in power was greater. As I made the changes, even though some of them were only temporary, I found that I became more alive to the prompting of the Spirit in the moment.

Ironically, my traditional daily devotional hour was actually beginning to get in the way of real communication with God. Patterns of rote habit had taken over where the give and take of real relationship should have been. Since then I've come to know God's presence in a new way. I later returned to a disciplined practice of daily meditative prayer, but it has new life and flexibility in it.

So, let God both destroy and rebuild your pattern for prayer and Scripture study, and don't let yourself feel guilty if it seems like you're not praying or studying at all for a time. Shut out those religious voices that tell you God will do nothing if you don't pray. God is simply not that small. If He had to be limited to responding to the puny actions I am able to take as a finite human being, my faith would be a sorry one indeed. Besides, your guilt will vanish when the newer, more adequate form emerges. Allow for experiment and failure in the meantime.

Begin breaking patterns by confessing your helplessness, and then call upon the Lord to rescue you. It's a time-honored and proven-to-bear-fruit cry.

7

LIVING WITH A THIRD STAGE BURNOUT VICTIM

In my situation, my wife escaped most of what I suffered and was able to support me in my recovery. Her invincibly positive nature forms a good counterbalance to my melancholy one and I write this chapter from the wellspring of her instinctive wisdom in dealing with me. The basic outline for this chapter is her work. I realize, however, that there are cases in which both husband and wife are suffering third stage incapacities. For their sakes I've done my best to address their situation as well as my own. Many of the support functions outlined here for a spouse can be effectively shouldered by a close friend, as well.

Let's begin with couples who are both wounded at the same time. The most basic temptation you face is to see one another as the enemy. You're no longer able to meet one another's needs. Mutual need becomes mutual demand. Demand disappointed becomes anger. Poorly processed anger makes lovers into enemies. Because even normal household pressures aren't adequately dealt with by either of you, they quickly grow from small irritations into very large ones. Chances are you've never been able to be real partners in the sharing of emotions anyway, even in your healthy days. The present situation, therefore, widens a hidden crack into a gaping chasm.

So, no matter how incapacitated you feel, the

first mental discipline you must strive to exercise is to identify the real enemy and resolve not to attack your mate. Your enemy is the situation you face, not your mate. If you can't yet face the situation together and learn to talk out your feelings with one another, then at least learn not to attack one another. I can't give you a multi-step plan for accomplishing this. You wouldn't be able to follow it anyway. I can only say that you must do it by God's grace, directly and simply. Get a trusted third party to help you do it, if necessary, but get it done. I myself have spent a number of hours interpreting wounded spouses to wounded spouses. It helps.

The burnout victim desperately needs his "space". "Down" time, spent alone, is crucial to his recovery, so be prepared to carry more than your share of the weight in the household, if he is wounded and you remain functional. He no longer has the capacity to deal effectively or consistently with daily stresses and responsibilities. It may seem to you that he will never rebound from his pain, but he will, unless you compound it with misunderstanding and misplaced pressures.

It will be a lonely time for you - a time for laying down your own life and your own needs - while one who may once have been strong limps through a period of weakness. Listen sympathetically to his hurts, fears, depressions and angers, but don't wallow in them with him. At all costs remain positive. He doesn't need the pressure you create by becoming angry with him or by insensitively demanding that he do things to correct his condition or his behavior.

Above all, *believe* in him when he can't believe in himself. Beth used to put herself directly in my face - the only time I could handle the pressure of direct frontal communication - and firmly tell me I was a good pastor, a good father and a good man. I needed to hear it. I knew too well that my performance at home was deteriorating, and I was encouraged as she helped me to hold onto my identity.

Your wounded one may have lost all faith that God will choose to conquer the situation. If this is the case, your job is to maintain faith on his behalf, no matter how difficult it may seem. The wounded one is hanging on by a decision of his will - "white-knuckling it", if he's hanging on at all - not feeling near to God or even believing that God is willing to help. If you can believe *for* him without preaching sermons about it, you help rebuild his faith.

If both of you are wounded, then, *as a couple,* find someone outside the marriage to do for you what one of you can no longer do for the other. It may be a time of distance in your relationship and is therefore a time of extraordinary vulnerability. Because of this vulnerability, under no circumstances should you seek help or support from a member of the opposite sex individually, outside the marriage. I scarcely need to spell out for you the dangers that lie down that path. Seek out that person or persons *together* and get help *jointly.* Best if you can find another couple. Better yet if you have a small group that meets regularly for prayer, ministry and fellowship. "Dump" there together. Let them believe in you and reaffirm your callings as individuals and as a couple.

If you are the whole one and your mate is wounded, do all you can to keep the household running smoothly. Maintain a light atmosphere, happy and orderly. The comfort and the refuge of home are a balm to the burnout victim. At this point in his life it's too easy for home to become a place of pressure that drives him outside to find "space" and peace. Remember how easily cognitive distortions can make things seem different than they are, how easily problems can be magnified out of proportion to reality through the filter of his pain. Outside the home, his vulnerability opens him to those who would prey upon his emotional need. Home must be a place where he knows he won't be wounded or poked.

If you find your burnout victim sitting alone in a stupor somewhere, eyes glazed, staring into space, gracefully leave him in it and deal with the household on your own. He'll be fine and eventually he'll come out of it. You'll only drive him further into withdrawal by making demands. You might even spark an angry outburst. Countless times Beth found me sitting at the kitchen table, staring into a plate of food or contemplating the grain of the wood in the table, lost to the world. A simple hug around the shoulders with no accompanying demand for response was medicine to my ailing spirit. She would then go on about her business, praying for me all the while, and I felt it.

If both of you are wounded, you must exercise as much self control as you are capable of. Again, I say that you must strive not to identify one another as the enemy. It may help to learn to recognize when the household pressure is building on the two of you and resolve to go out together for a while before one or both of you explodes. Get a sitter for the kids and go to a movie or take a walk. Anything to break the pattern and get out of the pressured environment.

In every case in which I have seen two burnout victims at war with one another in a marriage relationship, there were definitely deep-seated problems of another kind feeding into it. Those problems existed long before the wounding from outside the marriage began, and they only surfaced in force when the couple's normal restraining strengths wore thin. Remember that the pressure of burnout opens hidden cracks and exposes concealed weaknesses so that changes can be made.

By contrast, couples who are whole as individuals seem to survive well even when both parties are wounded. I believe that when mortal combat in the home accompanies burnout produced by outside forces, the ultimate source is often a wise and loving God who deliberately aggravates our brokenness so that we will take note, face the hidden issues and resolve them.

I've seen wounded couples in burnout do just this sort of facing of issues and not only survive, but come through it more whole and clean than before suffering forced the issue. In the facing of those issues, they were healed of old wounds and sins, and were then enabled to recover together from their present state of burnout..

If you are the whole one, cover your sufferer with a blanket of prayer every waking hour. It will give you a sense that you are helping, rather than standing helplessly by, and real power will be released to mend your partner's wounds. Don't encourage him in ways that demand performance, and don't tell him what you're praying for. He'll feel obligated for your sake to try to make it all happen, and that only deepens the condition.

When both of you are wounded, find someone outside of your marriage to pray this way for you, because neither of you will be able to do it consistently for one another. Make certain this person understands your condition, and then trust him. As I said before, never seek out that support as an individual alone if you can possibly act jointly. For safety's sake it should be done together. Best if you find a couple. Better yet if you have a small group of trusted friends in Christ with whom you meet regularly. They can share the burden and give much more effective support.

Out in the world, the healthy one in the relationship must keep a sharp lookout for what kinds of people are hanging around the wounded one. If your wounded one is a leader or a pastor, this is especially necessary in church where people press in on the leader, demanding ministry with no concept of, or care for, his personal condition. Begin by guarding his heart with prayer. With the help of Father God, be strong in your own spirit and, in an almost mystical way, carry the bleeding heart of your burnout victim in your own bosom. Lift his pain to the Father on his behalf. **Bear one another's burdens and so fulfill the law of Christ** (Galatians 6:2).

For instance, at church Beth might notice that a certain person known for being a "leech" had me cornered and was droning on and on while I turned ghastly shades of gray. In a case like that she would come quickly to my side in order to strengthen me silently with prayer. She formed a shield in the spirit. And I would be further strengthened simply by not being alone.

Beth also had a sixth sense concerning those who would take advantage of my vulnerability, that *Distant Early Warning System* I wrote about earlier. She warned me many times and I learned to heed her. I was free to listen or not to listen, and she didn't add to the pressure by insisting that I *act* like I had heard her. She simply stated the facts and then left me alone.

Often she'd head people off by getting to them herself before they could get to me. She'd do it so nicely and subtly that the potential troublemaker didn't even know what had happened. For all anyone else knew, she was just the usual friendly, happy Beth coming to visit.

Never do this sort of thing in an obvious way that lets the one you're heading off know you're angry or being protective. You'll only look bad in their eyes and create new tensions in the body of Christ that your wounded one will have to deal with later.

When both of you are wounded and in need of protection, I again advise you to alert trusted others to do for you what you may be unable to do for one another. You'll find, however, that even in the depth of wounding, those protective instincts remain active and functional. To a certain degree, you can continue to exercise protective functions for one another, no matter what condition you're in. I think this is so because a threat to your mate is perceived as a threat to yourself. In your wounding, your paranoia keeps alive those protective instincts. Up to a point those instincts are reliable. The problem for the burnout victim, however, is one of balance and a tendency to carry a sixth sense for trouble beyond the bounds of reality. Cognitive distortions quickly become full blown delusions if not watched carefully. Seek, therefore, to be disciplined enough not to turn the protective words you speak to your mate into demands that must be responded to. Then use the checks and balances provided by those trusted others I spoke of to control your own tendency to lose perspective.

If you're the functional one in the relationship, be acutely aware at all times that those who wounded your partner were probably trusted friends, people with whom he risked himself, people into whom he poured his time, love and energy. He's been stabbed in the back by them, and his heart is cut to ribbons. The problem may not be one of forgiveness. He may already have accomplished that. It's just that emotional woundings are much like physical ones.

They take time to heal, even after medicine is applied or the irritant removed. The process will probably take much longer to complete than you think you can bear, but it does run its course. Learn patience in the meantime. It is therefore of paramount importance that you not betray his confidence. Share with no one what he shares with you.

> **Let every one be on guard against his neighbor, And do not trust any brother; Because every brother deals craftily, And every neighbor goes about as a slanderer. And everyone deceives his neighbor, And does not speak the truth, They have taught their tongue to speak lies; They weary themselves committing iniquity. Your dwelling is in the midst of deceit; Through deceit they refuse to know Me, declares the Lord.** Jeremiah 9:4-6.

> **Even my close friend, in whom I trusted, Who ate my bread, Has lifted up his heel against me.** Psalm 41.

Deep wounds from betrayals such as these often take years to heal. As you conceal from others what your wounded one has shared with you, conceal his general condition as well. In every way help him preserve the public image of strong functionality before the world. *No one,* except those the burnout victim says are all right, need know how he really feels. If asked, say, "He's alright, but you can pray for us; it never hurts." Don't risk giving anyone ammunition that might be used later to add to the problem of wounding and burnout. Don't risk damaging your partner's trust in you. He may have no place else to go, and his trust in you can spell the difference between survival and complete breakdown.

While you are preserving a functional public image, take care not to undermine your partner's self-esteem by taking up *too* much of the slack he leaves, either at home, at work or in the ministry. Better to lend just a *little* help in the doing of a task than to do it *all* for him. Better even to let a task go undone than to add to his guilt burden by doing jobs he knows and accepts as his own.

Your own needs will have to be set aside for a while. The one in deep wounding isn't capable of meeting them. He'll try, but he really has nothing to work with. Your response to his incapacity can be either healing to him or immeasurably destructive. I know of one wife who - wounded by her husband's incapacity to meet her needs, and not understanding the reason for it - turned to the attack and accused him of everything from lack of love to hypocrisy in his faith and ministry. She pushed and pushed until he exploded. His raw nerves couldn't take the pressure. To show love, to pay attention to a new dress or to appreciate how well a household task was accomplished, is often beyond his capability. There is simply nothing left to give and no amount of spiritual or emotional grunting on his part will produce it. The burnout victim is fully aware of his failure. In fact, the guilt of it is driving him deeper into burnout, but there is almost nothing he can do to change it.

You'll have to learn to draw from the Lord alone what you need to sustain your own emotional health. If you have children in the home, you'll have to find the faith to believe that God knew what shape their wounded parent would be in and that He has already provided for their survival, turning all things to good (Romans 8:28). Sometimes I was so "gone" that the very presence of my wonderful children made me want to scream in desperation. Try as I might, I couldn't respond to them as they needed me to. Their little voices were like daggers cutting my mind in pieces and carving chunks off my already bleeding nerves.

Family members often had to repeat things to me two and three times in order to make their messages understood. I could hear the sound they made, but my mind couldn't make sense of what was being said. I would ask for things to be repeated again and again until the kids gave up and got Beth to tell me. I can still hear her carefully instructing, "Get in his face. Make certain you have eye contact. Ask him if he is listening. Then ask him to repeat what you said. If that doesn't work, come get me."

Beth was wise enough not to criticize me for my inability. She knew what kind of man I am under normal circumstances and was therefore able to give me room to recover. I gave to the children as I could, and I knew Beth covered for me when I couldn't. On the whole, however, she tells me I did well with the children. I knew that as children they could never understand what was happening to their father and so I made extra effort.

My son is twenty-two years old as I write. He's a burden bearer, incredibly prophetically sensitive to what's in other people. As a child of only eight and nine years, therefore, he sensed my exhaustion and decided in his own heart to make no demands of me, not to burden me with his own developing needs. He closed off from me emotionally and began to face his life crises without my help. Later, this vow not to burden me became a bitterness and a barrier between us that we've been working through together over the last couple of years. God is good. Burnout takes its toll on everyone associated with the burnout victim, but for every hurt, our Lord provides a means to heal.

Through it all Beth learned more deeply than ever how to derive her sense of self-worth and beauty from the Lord. She learned to sense when He noticed and when He complimented her at the times when I couldn't. She "embraced her fireball" in the form of her own loneliness - as I embraced mine - and let it work purification in her heart to drive her directly to her Lord. As a result, she outgrew the need for me to supply those things I could no longer supply. Then, when I did begin to recover, and did begin to affirm and to nurture her again, she was delighted, but not dependent.

Most what I've written here comes from the perspective of a man supported by his wife. I need to emphasize that when the wife is wounded and the husband is functional, the task is exactly the same. Husband and wife are partners in ministry and the partnership must be defended. It isn't that Beth's and my relationship is more important than our ministry, but rather that our ministry is first to both of us as a centerpiece of our union. We minister together in partnership. In fact, our ministry is a big part of why our marriage works so well. We're like warriors who fight back to back, guarding one another from attack even as we advance and take ground from the adversary. When one goes down, the other stands guard so that the partnership is preserved. Neither of us works as well alone as we do together.

In 1984 Beth and I were scheduled to teach and lead worship at a national gathering of the renewal movement in the denomination we were then a part of. Just a few days before our scheduled departure, however, Beth was admitted to the hospital with acute abdominal pain. A day later, surgeons removed a cyst the size of grapefruit from her left fallopian tube, which had twisted and become gangrenous due to loss of blood supply. It was a major surgery. After the surgery she almost died from an allergic reaction to morphine. but the crisis passed. I could have gone on to the meeting and Beth would have been okay in the hospital, but the Holy Spirit clearly told me not to go. I was to stay home and guard my wounded partner for the sake of our love and our ministry together, and so for three days I spent every spare moment sitting in the hospital holding her hand.

I've been amazed to discover how many ministers' wives are suffering at home because of tongues wagging in criticism for the way she carries herself in the church. In many fellowships the minister's spouse does as much work as he does and in nearly every aspect of the ministry. She, too, can burn out in the service of the Lord and needs the same care her husband would need if he were wounded. Unfortunately, too many husband/pastors have no sense of partnership and so neglect the wounded one on the home front. They often continue to pursue their ministries, all but blind to the plight of their mates. Some of my current staff are licensed and ordained women. I pray first that they don't burn out under my leadership, and second that their husbands are as supportive of them as my wife has been of me.

Finally, in no way take personal responsibility for your wounded mate's recovery. What he is suffering is an issue to be settled ultimately between him and his Lord. You can pray, support, love and listen. You can avoid being part of the problem and you can help by creating an environment conducive to healing, but in the end you may not turn out to be a key part of the solution. The solution can only be found between him and his Father God. They're the ones who must settle the issues. Grant him the room to hash it out within himself without joining him in his bitterness, preaching at him or offering unsolicited counsel.

The result in your recovered partner will be increased wisdom, balance, stability, power and all the fruits of the Spirit. It's worth waiting for.

8

LINGERING QUESTIONS

How long will my recovery take?

Speed of recovery depends on a number of factors. How healthy were you before you sank into burnout? How strong is your general make-up, both physically and emotionally? What kind of support systems are available to you to aid and assist in your healing? What kinds of pressures continue to drain your energies? Is good counsel available? Under any circumstances, recovery is usually a lengthy process. It takes months or even years for the deeply burned out to return to strength, so prepare yourself emotionally for a long period of struggle. You've spent resources that are not easily replaced and you must give yourself time to rebuild them.

Will I recover completely?

Yes and no. You will probably never fully recover the level of intensity, strength and resilience you enjoyed before you burned out. Unfortunately, you have squandered an only partially renewable resource and you will henceforth and forever be compelled to measure your limited strength against the tasks that come your way. You will, however, have gained a wisdom more valuable and more life-giving than the resources you lost. You may, therefore, actually become more productive with less expenditure of energy than you thought possible. You will also discover that you are much less easily driven off balance emotionally. Your sense of perspective will have been honed to a razor edge.

What about relapses?

You'll have many in the course of your recovery. For a long time, if I over-extended myself for too long a period of time, I would suddenly feel completely undone, as if there had been no recovery at all. Such episodes mean little. Rest and a stronger sense of perspective tend to cure me.

For a while you may feel like a bouncing ball, sometimes in the depths of your former despair, sometimes out. Or you may descend to stage one and then recover quickly, only to plunge to the very bottom a week later. Having done so, you may awaken the next morning wondering what the whole thing was about, after all, because you feel so great again. Remember that recovery takes time and that temporary relapses are part of the process.

What if my mate thinks that all this is just a bunch of nonsense and won't stop putting pressure on me to perform what I can no longer perform?

This is not an uncommon problem, especially for female victims. Too many husbands don't understand the condition and often don't even *wish* to understand. Because of this they continue making selfish demands upon the wife's emotional and physical energy, condemning her if she can't produce, and ultimately placing her in danger of serious breakdown. The problem can happen to men, as well, but the victims of this kind of spousal refusal to understand are most often women.

Much of my answer to this question is included in the previous chapter, but I'll add one more dimension here. As a last resort when a mate refuses to come to terms with your need, a temporary separation may be in order until you have had time to regain your strength and balance. The pain of your absence may serve to bring about needed humility and understanding in your mate, and you will find the space you must have to begin rebuilding your lost strength.

Set aside any legalisms you may have accumulated concerning God's command that married people should stay together no matter what. You're doing this *in order that* you might be able to remain together. In fact, if you don't get some distance, the alternative may be forced separation in the form of extended hospitalization.

Wives in burnout, forget all those misapplied Scriptures about wifely submission. This has little to do with the issue of submission, but rather with recovering enough strength so that you are able once again to actively submit, one to another (Ephesians 5:21 and following), in effective partnership.

Why did God let this happen to me?
Read on......

PART II

THE DARK NIGHT OF THE SOUL

I am a warrior
I have fought long
Until the sweat stings my eyes
And tears choke my battle cry
Fight on!

When youth's exuberance and morning's hope
bleed red upon the ground
Then wisdom's steady hand keeps on.

Sweat-burned eyes do see
While tear-choked throat soars free in song.
What must be done
What must be sung
I win because I cannot lose.
I live for I have learned to die.

Loren Sandford, 3/96

9
THE DARK NIGHT OF THE SOUL

After my time of burnout, I was granted a couple of good years of recovered health and strength before a new chapter began, one more painful than I could have dreamed. A beloved foster family in our church had adopted thirteen "unadoptable" children, in addition to their own four by birth. They were arrested in Virginia while on an extended trip as a family and were charged with the murder of one of the children. They were convicted and imprisoned. One of my trusted staff members committed adultery with three women in the church and had to be dismissed. We built a building with a loan from our denomination, fell behind in payments and then were forced to withdraw from the denomination because of apostate actions General Synod was taking. I had to fire a youth pastor for serious errors in judgment. A fallen pastor who had been with us for healing and restoration left to plant a church six miles away and took a block of people with him. Each of these crises cost us in uncounted ways and affected us more deeply - and me more personally - than I can begin to say here.

As a result of all these crises and a host of lesser ones, the heart was blown out of our church. We began losing members. Elders began to leave, burned out and exhausted over the long years of struggle, and angry with me in ways and for issues that made no sense to me at the time. I was personally audited by the IRS and, because of the incompetence of my tax accountant and my own willingness to remain ignorant of what he was doing, I was assessed $8500 in back taxes and interest at a time when an assesment like that could have sent me into bankruptcy. The news of the results came while I was away on an extended ministry trip. Then both of my girls were sexually assaulted while I was away on the same ministry trip, unable to get home to be their strength in the situation.

During the same period of time, after months and months of struggle, I finally decided to leave my home of twelve years, where my entire family lived (father, mother, siblings, etc.), resign the church I had planted and pastored for most of that time, and move to Denver to become the executive pastor of a mega-church. Contrary to what had been presented during the negotiation stage, the system there was in trouble. I was presented as the "step-father" to replace the senior pastor who wanted to be free to pursue his music career without really letting go of the church. People were angry at his absence and disturbed by a host of other issues. I represented a poor attempt to mollify them. They really didn't buy it and I really can't blame them. For many of the same reasons, staff didn't buy it either, and I found my most precious values either thrust aside or, in some cases, ridiculed. Even if the senior pastor had been able to release what needed to be released, it was simply a bad fit. I didn't belong, and by the time it was over, every good gift I had ever had confidence in had been maligned, from my preaching and teaching to my music. I resigned after just fourteen months.

I spent three hellish months - unemployed and under a hail of gunfire - carefully discerning the Lord's will for my future, afraid I'd led my family and myself into a terrible dead end. The move had been hard on them, especially on my oldest daughter. I felt their pain acutely. All of this crisis was only the beginning of a time of crushing more deep and furious than I could have imagined during the burnout years. In the end, a series of miracles and signs confirmed the Lord's guidance to plant a new church in the north end of the Denver metro area.

There are times when burnout feels as if you're hanging onto the edge of a cliff by your fingernails, afraid that you'll fall and that God won't be there to catch you. In the wilderness, or dark night of the soul, you plead, "God, if I suffer any more, I'll break," and He says, "Right!" End of discussion. Your fingernails snap and you do fall off the cliff, only to find out it's bottomless and that God really isn't there to catch you. At least that's how you feel, and no one can convince you otherwise.

The dark night of the soul is a time in which there seems to be no sense of the presence or blessing of God. It's a time of exposure to the onslaught of repeated disaster with little or no perception of His protection, or even His presence. Nothing works. You're a failure in all you try.

It was a time in which God would send me to do a thing, confirm the direction miraculously, and then not meet me there. He would withhold the provision I needed to accomplish the task and then leave me alone to struggle with it. We built that magnificent building in Post Falls in the midst of miracle. We qualified for a loan sufficient only to build a functional shell with no furnishings, but God actually gave us a completely finished and furnished facility with a lighted parking lot. The loan itself was a one-in-ten shot. I expected the miracle to continue. God had ordered it and confirmed it; God would pay for it, but within a few months we were $25,000 behind in mortgage payments. I would hire staff based on current income and clear needs, only to see that income dry up. I cut expenses to relieve budget deficits, only to see giving fall in direct proportion to the cuts. I didn't understand. I felt abandoned, even betrayed by both people and God. Then followed all the other disasters. In the midst of it, my health took a serious turn for the worse. Nothing in my life was left untouched.

Quitting was never a live option. I knew that. I am who I am and I do what I do. I had burned my bridges to other kinds of labor and lifestyle too long ago to re-evaluate now. With or without the sense of His presence, and whether or not He seemed to prosper my life and work, I would therefore serve the Lord.

In the late 17th and early 18th centuries, Madame Guyon, living in France, persecuted and imprisoned by the church, wrote of her own experience of the dark night of the soul:

There comes a time in the believer's life when the Lord withdraws the joy. He will seemingly

115

withdraw the graces. At the same time, the Christian may also find himself in a period of persecution - persecution, no less, than that coming from Christians in religious authority. Further, he may find much difficulty in his home or private life. He may also be experiencing great difficulties with his health. Somewhere there will be a great deal of pain or other losses too numerous to mention. The believer may also be undergoing experiences which he feels are totally unique to himself. Other Christians, in whom he has put his trust, may forsake him and mistreat him. He may feel that he has been very unjustly treated. He will feel this toward men and he will feel it toward his God, for - in the midst of all this other pain and confusion - it will seem that God, too, has left him!

Even more believers give up the journey when the Lord seems to have forsaken them in the spirit and left their spirit dead - while the world and all else is crashing in on them, friends forsaking them, and great suffering and pain abounding everywhere in their lives. .... But the true land of promise always lies beyond a vast wasteland. Promise is found only on the far side of a desert....... When you can go beyond that place and not seeing your Lord, believe He is there by the eyes of faith alone; when you can walk further and further into Christ when there are no senses, no feelings, not even the slightest registration of the presence of God; when you can sit before Him when everything around you and within you seems to be either falling apart or dead; and when you can come before your Lord without question and without demand, serene in faith alone, and there, before Him, worship Him without distraction, without a great deal of consciousness of self and with no spiritual sense of Him, then will the test of commitment begin to be established. Then will begin the true journey of the Christian life. (From <u>Final Steps in Christian Maturity</u>, Madame Jeanne Guyon, Christian Books Publishing House, 1985).

I have a passion for testing everything by the Word of God. It isn't enough for me just to see that someone somewhere in the history of the church experienced and then explained a thing. It isn't even enough that I myself might experience that same thing. I have committed myself to ask, "Is such an experience to be found in the Scripture?" In this case, the answer is unequivocally, yes. Aside from Job's trials, which we'll look at in a later chapter, the dark night of the soul is perfectly described in Psalm 88, the only psalm in the Bible without a shred of clear hope. It contains the unvarnished desperation and despair of the author, together with the single most important component for successfully navigating that time of desolation.

Verses 1-3, **O LORD, the God of my salvation, I have cried out by day and in the** night before Thee. Let my prayer come before Thee; Incline Thine ear to my cry! For my soul has had enough of troubles, And my life has drawn near to Sheol. Suffering had gone on so long, and had affected him so deeply, the psalmist could absorb no more. He felt as if he were about to die and wished to do so.

Verse 4, **I am reckoned among those who go down to the pit; I have become like a man without strength.** People who knew him believed him to be afflicted by some kind of curse from God. He was seen as a man on his way to hell who must have been doing something wrong to be suffering like this. The stress of his suffering and the opinions of his friends and loved ones took such a toll on him physically that he could no longer count on health and strength for the living of life. He was broken and desolate physically, emotionally and spiritually.

Verse 5, **Forsaken among the dead, Like the slain who lie in the grave, Whom Thou dost remember no more, And they are cut off from Thy hand.** God had forgotten him. He'd lost his sense of the Lord's presence. He reached out, but God wasn't there. Cut off from his sense of the Lord's life-giving presence, He felt as if he had already died, though his heart still beat in his chest.

Verse 6, **Thou hast put me in the lowest pit, In dark places, in the depths.** The psalmist knew beyond a doubt that his hurt and desolation were the hand of God. During this period in my own life, I served on the faculty of a three week counseling school in Maryland. During a question-

and-answer time, a question arose concerning the dark night of the soul. I stated that I knew the hand of God was against me and that nothing I did would prosper until He chose to make it so. It raised quite a controversy, but the psalmist clearly tells us, *God has put me in this place.*

Verse 7, **Thy wrath has rested upon me, And Thou hast afflicted me with all Thy waves.** He was certain God was angry with him over some hidden trespass, otherwise God would not send such suffering. The image is of a man struggling in a relentless high surf, exhausted by the pounding of the waves. Every time he nearly succeeds in gaining his footing, yet another wall of water strikes him down and rolls him under in the sand and grit of the beach, filling his mouth and nostrils with salt. Coughing and retching, he rises, only to be driven under, time and time again. Disaster after disaster. Hurt upon hurt.

Verse 8, **Thou hast removed my acquaintances far from me; Thou hast made me an object of loathing to them; I am shut up and cannot go out.** No one could bear to be around him anymore. Other believers were frightened, even repulsed by the intensity and the duration of his suffering. He was profoundly alone with no one to truly understand his condition. So overcome was he with grief, trouble and fatigue that he couldn't even bring himself to venture out on the streets. I've been there. I understand. There were times I couldn't control the shaking of my hands and simply stayed home, locked up in my home office, unable to go out and face the world.

Verse 9, **My eye has wasted away because of affliction; I have called upon Thee every day, O Lord; I have spread out my hands to Thee.** As in Madame Guyon's account, still the psalmist sought His God. Still he prayed and held his heart open to the presence of the Most High. Even when there seemed to be no response and no relief, he kept at it in a disciplined way, **every day**.

Verse 10, **Wilt Thou perform wonders for the dead? Will the departed spirits rise and praise Thee?** Sarcasm and anger began to surface. Relentless and senseless pain and suffering sometimes reduce us to that. *So you want to be praised, Lord? How can I do that if I'm dead? Is that what you want?* I stayed angry a long time, but the intensity of my own experience eventually burned that out of me and I learned to submit to whatever God was sending.

Verses 11-12, **Will Thy lovingkindness be declared in the grave, Thy faithfulness in Abaddon? Will Thy wonders be made known in the darkness and Thy righteousness in the land of forgetfulness?**

Verse 13, **But I, O Lord, have cried out to Thee for help. And in the morning my prayer comes before Thee.** *No matter what I suffer, no matter how far away You seem and no matter how angry I may become at Your distance, Lord, yet I pray. I seek Your presence.* Perseverance is essential to survival in the dark night. Stay with the ministry. Keep serving Him.

Maintain worship. Study the Word. Don't break your stride. When all is such fog and blindness that you can't even see your hand before your face, choose, by an act of the will, to trust the eternal compass and walk on. Even if it feels all wrong, it *will* be right.

Verse 14, **O Lord, why dost Thou reject my soul? Why dost Thou hide Thy face from me?** I repeat, the dark night is a time of seeming abandonment and even rejection, a time when God blesses by *not* blessing. The mystery of redemptive suffering and fear!

Verse 15, **I was afflicted and about to die from my youth on; I suffer Thy terrors; I am overcome.** For the psalmist, this had been going on for a long time. Too long. Even from adolescence. He was worn down by it, helpless before the onslaught of his suffering.

Verses 16-17, **Thy burning anger has passed over me; Thy terrors have destroyed me. They have surrounded me like water all day long; They have encompassed me altogether.** *I am drowning. The water has gone over my head. I am helpless. I am dying. And you've done it, Lord. You're responsible. You've brought this fear of mine out into the light and now it's out of control.*

Verse 18, **Thou hast removed lover and friend far from me; My acquaintances are in darkness.** The dark night is a time of profound loneliness. No one understands. No one hears. People give rotten advice based on hurtful misunderstandings and cheap theology. In order to avoid the sting of their misguided wisdom, you begin to hide from people. Because those who suffer in this way are seldom any fun to be around, friendships gradually erode. In the face of their own powerlessness to help, people flee. And that is where we leave the psalmist. Without friends. Without hope. Without praise. Knowing only that his gnawing hunger for God rages unabated, he maintains the discipline of daily seeking God, no matter how deaf or distant the heavens may seem.

What does this mean? What is its purpose? The answer is preparation. God is preparing a new move of His Spirit. I realize there is a spreading renewal just now, but I don't think the current renewal is "it", although I do believe the present outpouring is laying the groundwork for the "main event" to come later. I think it will take a form we haven't seen before. I don't believe it will focus so much on signs and wonders as on the gentle compassion of Jesus and His mercy. Signs and wonders of an order never seen before will manifest, but they'll be eclipsed by an even more important revival of the character of Jesus shining through His people.

I believe this will be a revival in, of and for the church, more than just a wave that breaks and is gone again, but a time in which the Holy Spirit will descend and *remain* because of what God has done to prepare the foundation in His bride, *and most especially her leadership.* I believe a great many of us are being prepared by means of what St.

John of the Cross called the dark night of the soul. It is what Madame Guyon spoke of in the quote above, and what the author of Psalm 88 lamented in his hurt and abandonment.

A people is being prepared together with a generation of leadership that I believe has been largely held back and hidden until now. That leadership has been going to school, so to speak, and I believe some of them are graduating. They've been led into the wilderness while everyone else was having fun. They've wept while others laughed, and lost out while others prospered. As confusing as it's been, in that brokenness they've been learning to love as Jesus loved. They've been working through their own sharing of the cross of Christ and His resurrection, becoming more one with Jesus than they had ever understood or experienced before, both in His death and in His life.

Pathema is a New Testament Greek word that means "suffering", but suffering of a particular kind. It is the suffering which is necessary to the calling. It means that if you would accept the calling, you must accept the suffering that comes with it and is the price for it. Those who refuse the suffering, can't attain the calling.

Some occurrences of *pathema* in Scripture:

Romans 8:18, **For I consider that the *sufferings* of this present time are not worthy to be compared with the glory that is to be revealed to us.**

II Corinthians 1:5, **For just as the** *sufferings* **of Christ are ours in abundance, so also our comfort is abundant through Christ.**

II Corinthians 1:6, **But if we are afflicted, it is for your comfort and salvation; or if we are comforted, it is for your comfort, which is effective in the patient enduring of the same** *sufferings* **which we also suffer.**

II Corinthians 1:7, **For we do not want you to be unaware, brethren, of our** *affliction* **which came to us in Asia, that we were burdened excessively, beyond our strength, so that we despaired even of life.**

Philippians 3:10, **that I may know Him, and the power of His resurrection and the fellowship of His** *sufferings,* **being conformed to His death.**

Colossians 1:24, **Now I rejoice in my** *sufferings* **for your sake, and in my flesh I do my share on behalf of His body (which is the church) in filling up that which is lacking**

in Christ's afflictions.

II Timothy 3:11, **persecutions, and** *sufferings*, **such as happened to me at Antioch, at Iconium and at Lystra; what persecutions I endured, and out of them all the Lord delivered me!**

Hebrews 2:9, **But we do see Him who has been made for a little while lower than the angels, namely Jesus, because of the** *suffering* **of death crowned with glory and honor, that by the grace of God He might taste death for everyone.**

Hebrews 2:10, **For it was fitting for Him, for whom are all things, and through whom are all things, in bringing many sons to glory, to perfect the author of their salvation through** *sufferings*.

Hebrews 10:32, **But remember the former days, when, after being enlightened, you endured a great conflict of** *sufferings*.

I Peter 1:11, **seeking to know what person or time the Spirit of Christ** within them was indicating as He predicted the *sufferings* of Christ and the glories to follow.

I Peter 4:13, **but to the degree that you share the *sufferings* of Christ, keep on rejoicing; so that also at the revelation of His glory, you may rejoice with exultation.**

I Peter 4:1-2 is important, **Therefore, since Christ has *suffered* in the flesh, arm yourselves also with the same purpose, because he who has *suffered* in the flesh has ceased from sin, so as to live the rest of the time in the flesh no longer for the lusts of men, but for the will of God.**

Scripture shows us a repeated pattern in which a man first receives a call, experiences success, is driven into exile and then finally returns to fulfill his destiny in the Lord. *Pathema* is essential to the process. For example, Joseph was called to lead his brothers (calling) and was given powerful gifts of prophecy (success). Unbroken, arrogant and immature, he tried them out on his brothers, created offense and was sold into slavery (exile). Later, in Egypt, he rose to power, his true destiny, and was able to minister to his family in a time of famine (return).

David was anointed king by the prophet Samuel (calling). Through military victory he achieved prominence in Saul's court and received the praise of the people (success), only to be driven into the wilderness by Saul's jealous insanity (exile). Yet it was he who, after Saul's death, united the tribes and established a stable monarchy (return). Destiny follows the dark night. The dark night of exile prepares the servant for destiny.

New Testament Saul, who later became Paul, was converted (calling) and immediately began preaching in Damascus, leading many to Christ (success), but he was driven from the city and spent fourteen years in the Arabian wilderness (exile). Finally, as he was living in Tarsus and making tents for a living, the eldership of Antioch sent for him, and it was they who ultimately launched him on his missionary journeys (return).

In each case there was calling and initial success, followed by exile (wilderness) and then a return and entrance into the true destiny. We're summoned, given a taste of our gifting and then sent to the crucible of suffering and exile where our character is rearranged and refined. The end is that, having been prepared by means of a baptism of extended fire, we're called back to service and into our true destiny. The promised land always lies on the far side of a vast wilderness.

Many of those called to play key roles in the coming outpouring must also be prepared and then deployed by that same pattern. After enjoying times of initial success and anointing, we must undergo a wilderness exile of suffering in which we share the cross of Christ to a greater degree than the average Christian is ever asked to. Each of us called in this way must in some form, or variety of forms, suffer the **loss of all things** in order that we may gain Christ (Philippians 3). Those who won't take the cross can't take the calling.

I once made the mistake of saying to a prophetic friend of mine that I thought ten years of suffering was long enough. That was a long time ago and I had a long way to go. He laughed at me in a fatherly way and said, in his Oklahoma southern drawl, "Ten years ain't nothin'! I been sufferin' *twenty* years. I *like* sufferin'! When I'm sufferin', then I get to be with Jesus!" It was one of the gentler slaps in the face I've ever received, and, after I wrestled with it for a while - it wasn't what I had wanted to hear! - I took it to heart.

We need a *lifestyle* of brokenness, to take up the cross daily and follow Him. *And we need the mercy of God for a revelation of His person and compassion that is available to us only on the other side of the cross.* Because of the wilderness, like Paul, I no longer care to know anything except Jesus Christ, and Him crucified.

There is no more important lesson in this period of time than learning to abide in Jesus. That's what the dark night teaches us most deeply and indelibly. The dark night reveals His nature to us and in us. It takes us out of ourselves and plants us in Him.

Because of the dark night of the soul, I'm no

longer much concerned with teaching us how to prophesy, or heal, or learn new truths, or wield the gifts of the Spirit. It's all so much simpler than that, and accepting titles like "prophet" or "apostle" or "healer" is so distracting. Those titles seem to me too much like the match that lights the gasoline of my ambition and pride. They frighten me. It's really all about abiding in Him, as opposed to abiding in the ministry, or in the manifestations of the Spirit, or in some kind of doctrine. In Jesus are hid *all* the treasures.

I know a man who once asked the Lord how long the suffering had to go on, and the Lord replied, "Until there is nothing left to insult, nothing left to humiliate, nothing left to defend..." Embrace what God is sending and let it work its work. Do it desperately because desperately is how deeply we need it!

Hebrews 4:9-10, **There remains therefore a sabbath rest for the people of God. For the one who has entered His rest has himself also rested from his works, as God did from His.** God is bringing us to the end of our own works. In that kind of rest, He'll do mighty things in our midst that we haven't even imagined, and it will seem to us just a natural walk with Jesus as we simply do what He is doing. God help us who become impressed with our own giftedness as if it were our own! There lies danger!

Out of this weakness created by God flows the true, clean and pure mercy of Jesus for which the lost and wounded hunger so desperately. We, in the end time church (if, in fact, these are the end times in which we live), must be a people of mercy above all else. Nothing else will do. Only the mercy of Jesus has the power to overcome and heal the overwhelming hurt and destruction this sinful world has brought upon itself.

The dark night of the soul has nine purposes. **ONE:** *To bring about abandonment of any hope of personal reward for loving or serving God.* Luke 17:7-10 speaks of the slave who gets no praise for merely doing what he was ordered to do. It must be enough for us simply to know that we've done as our Lord has asked, no matter the outcome, or apparent lack of it. As long as some hope of personal reward survives to motivate our service, it colors what we do, how we do it and what kind of energy we put into the doing of it.

We've all suffered at the hands of "the prophet" who comes with a good word, but has a defiling delivery because of his need for self-validation. We've seen those prophetic "healers" who, for the same reason, promise healing that never materializes. We know the foul reek of ambition and the destruction wrought in the body of Christ by the need for recognition that fuels it. God desires a generation of leaders and servants to hear and serve clearly and cleanly so they can speak and act accurately and compassionately in His name. He needs for us to value serving Him above the thrill we get from doing it. *Pathema* with our Lord is the singular doorway to that rested place.

TWO: *To expose and purify defects by breaking them.* In fact, the purpose of the dark night is to expose everything about you as defective. You will appear stripped of every virtue. Romans 7:18, **For I know that nothing good dwells in me; that is, in my flesh; for the wishing is present in me, but the doing of the good is not.** We're not basically good people who somehow got broken and are going to be fixed by Jesus. We're thoroughly sinful people who must be crucified *with* Him. There were times during that dark night when I found myself in situation after situation in which I had to make a choice, but no matter what choice I made, I would appear to have broken my word. No matter what I did, I could not act with apparent integrity. I felt stripped of virtue with no way out. Why did God put me in such a position? Because it was crucial for me to realize that I didn't have it in my flesh even to walk with basic integrity without His help. It was important for me, like the apostle Paul, to come to despise every sense of self-goodness I had ever borne. I knew that everything I had ever done or produced, no matter how good, had been tainted with sin. **Nothing good dwells in me...**

THREE: *To bring about abandonment and despair of self*, a complete and accurate assessment of your own total depravity and the depth and magnitude of God's grace to cover it. When I have accepted and confessed the true depth of my sin, no accusation levelled at me can have any real force. I become unassailably secure, at rest in the totality of the forgiveness and grace I have been given. Romans

8:1, There is therefore now no condemnation for those who are in Christ Jesus. When I know and accept my condition, and understand God's grace in relation to it, there is nothing left to threaten. I can rest in Him only when I've despaired of me.

FOUR: *To bring about a faith that is without agenda or demand of God by means of breaking every dream and every hope.* The apostle Paul had learned to be content in all circumstances (Philippians 4:11). It all pays the same, whether I stand before a thousand or ten, whether I'm rich or poor, imprisoned or free. It must be the same joy, whether I play my music for five thousand or for a coffee house audience of two. Or will I follow Him if my problems *don't* evaporate? Am I His even if my dreams all fail? Will I serve and obey Him even if no prophetic word spoken over my life *ever* comes to pass? Or is it all somehow conditional? Is God blessing me only when things go well, or is His blessing equally present when the world is crashing down around my ears? Can I have the faith to see and understand that mystery?

FIVE: *To bring to rest the higher functions of the spirit.* Ease of movement in the Spirit. Hearing God. Perceiving Him. Jesus shining in and through us. While we are unbroken, these functions are always colored by personal agendas and desires, the ways we try to manipulate God to get what we think we need. Manipulation is based on unbelief that God will really honor His promise to *give* us what we need. Pure hearing comes only in and through the presence of faith in the absence of personal agenda or demand.

SIX: *To bring about a love for God which passes beyond loving Him for what He has done, or will do for us.* We need a love for God which passes beyond the reward we get from feeling it. Do I love God because it *feels* good to do so, or do I love Him for His own sake? The dark night brings us to the end of, *I love you ,God, because...* It teaches us a love for God that loves Him when there is no strength left to love and when there is no perception of His touch. The psalmist in Psalm 88 reached out to God morning by morning in love, even in the midst of despair.

SEVEN: *To bring about a purity of fellowship with Him.* Philippians 3:10, **that I may know Him and the power of His resurrection and the** *fellowship of His sufferings.*

EIGHT: *Humility* resulting in defenselessness, based on security in Jesus, leading to vulnerability and transparency. I came to a point where I could actually let nerds minister to me. I understood that I actually needed them. I could let my sins and weaknesses show and openly admit them even before crowds of people because I no longer needed to defend all those tender places inside of me. In burnout, I protected myself. I find that is no longer necessary and people seem to sense the openness. I'm more transparent and vulnerable than I have ever been, but people no longer seem to use

133

what I share against me as they once did. They sense instead that I am *with* them. Freedom, for both me and the people I serve, comes when I am no longer the slave of my own self image.

NINE: *Radical compassion* because I can truly, at last, identify with sinners, having been made to face and accept my own failure. The dark night brings about cross-centered, compelling compassion. The dark night destroys judgmentalism in every form and in every root.

10
THE NEW LEADERSHIP

For most of the thirty-nine years I've spent in and around charismatic renewal (I was seven when my parents brought it home), we were focused on learning new tools for ministry, new truths and new ways to be personally healed or made more whole. As time passed, too much of the movement degenerated into a giant self-improvement club reflecting the values of a self-centered society sometimes more than the love of God, or our love *for* God.

As a result, for a long time we were rather lost in the gifts of the Spirit, as if those gifts were the focal point of our Christian life, rather than the reality, the nature and the presence of Jesus. Many of us used our gifts as platforms to further our personal kingdoms and ambitions, and until very recently, it seemed God was letting us get away with it. Up to a point, His grace does cover a multitude of sins.

However, if we are to fully participate in the dawning glory, we must understand much more deeply than we ever have that the gifts of the Spirit aren't about us. They're about Jesus and His nature. They're tools for delivering His compassion to the needy, the broken and the lost. The longer I live, the more convinced I am that true compassion flows consistently only from a broken spirit and a contrite heart (Psalm 51:17), and that a broken spirit and a contrite heart are most often brought about through a wilderness of redemptive suffering, a dark night of the soul. Only the broken and contrite heart can fully, wisely and most effectively use the tools.

The problem is that the modern church has mostly lost the concept of redemptive suffering. Society conditions us to regard suffering or pain in any form as illegal, and we spend millions of dollars annually trying to anesthetize it. As a result, we too often teach that all pain is of the devil and therefore must be avoided or cast out, but this teaching is culturally conditioned, not biblically sound. It fails to represent the whole counsel of God, either in Scripture, or in the experience of the saints and martyrs throughout history.

There is a suffering which is the hand of God creating brokenness in His servant, bringing the flesh to death, creating dependence on Him, humility and wisdom. That kind of suffering must be embraced, cherished and accepted.

Often, when speaking of His own sufferings, Paul used the word, *pathema*, in the Greek, as I mentioned in the last chapter. *Pathema* is a kind of suffering to be accepted as unavoidable, part of the inevitable price, the *sine qua non* of high calling. He used *pathema*, for instance, in Philippians 3:10 when He spoke of knowing not only the power of the Lord's resurrection, but also the, "fellowship of His sufferings." Oneness with Jesus can never be complete apart from sharing the fullness of His experience, which includes redemptive suffering. One does not accept the calling of God to discipleship without at the same time accepting the price of that calling. Pray as you may, God will do nothing to relieve *pathema* until it produces what He intends it to produce in us. To relieve it prematurely would be to cheat both us and His kingdom.

In short, if you want to play football, you must run the laps. If you wish to earn the scholarship, you must choose to study. Redemptive suffering is the price God's servants pay for the glory of sharing in the compassionate nature of Jesus and the exercise of His power. But unlike in competitive sports, we cannot "achieve" *pathema*. We can only embrace it and submit to it, letting it work its work in us. We cannot gain the compassion of Jesus by developing it through human effort. We gain it by sharing in the death of Jesus, by submitting to it, in order that we might attain His life.

This is to say that all who are called to high calling in these present days must undergo some form of wilderness, or dark night of the soul, brought about by the hand of God, which is usually marked, at least in part, by a profound awareness of our individual human failure and our grief over it. On the night before the crucifixion - and rather full of himself - Peter, the apostle-in-training, boasted that he'd die with Jesus if need be. A few hours later, when the soldiers came to Gethsemane to arrest his Lord, Peter knew exactly what to do! Ready to die gloriously as a warrior fighting by Jesus' side, he drew steel and struck at the servant of the high priest, only to be rebuked by Jesus.

Later that same night, brave Peter three times denied he had ever known the Lord. Dying in battle was a thing he understood, but dying on a cross and sharing the humiliation and shame of it was a mystery he found himself unprepared to comprehend. The wonder of redemption is that before Peter could lead effectively in power with the heart and nature of his Lord, he had to know not his power, but his weakness and his desperate need for a Savior. The night before the crucifixion was a test I believe God *intended* Peter to fail. Paradoxically, his failure qualified him to lead.

> Luke 22:31-32, **Simon, Simon, Behold, Satan has demanded permission to sift you like wheat; but I have prayed for you, that your faith may not fail; and you, when once you have turned again, strengthen your brothers.**

Those who know, and have embraced, their own weakness have been freed to walk in the good clean strength of their Lord. Out of Peter's failure, compassion flowed to strengthen his brothers. Power and authority flow best upon a bed of compassion arising from brokenness of spirit, which is simply the failure of confidence in things human.

Jesus said that many are called and few are chosen (Matthew 22:14). If salvation comes by faith alone and not by works, then what does this passage mean? What is the difference between the called and the chosen? Are only a few destined to be saved?

Three main groups of people surrounded Jesus

in His earthly ministry. First came the multitude. They believed in Jesus, howbeit imperfectly, and by reason of that faith, they were saved. The foundation of their faith arose from their own personal needs for healing and deliverance, and their perception that Jesus could fulfill them, but it was faith nonetheless. Figuratively speaking, they played the part of the consumers in the ministry of Jesus, following after Him only because He sold a product for which they felt a hunger. They had faith in Him because He met their personal needs better than anything else currently available to them.

After the multitude, came the seventy who were identified as disciples. They followed Jesus wherever He went and eventually were sent out on a missionary journey, two by two. They followed Him because of high calling and because they had been chosen and called to serve, rather than to consume. A disciple is differentiated from the multitude by his active participation in giving the ministry of Jesus to those who have need. The disciples delivered the "product" the multitude had come for.

Finally there were the twelve closest to Him, destined to play key roles in the later development of the church. Their proximity to Jesus equipped them for a much greater exercise of authority than the others. Their destiny was to lead and mold the church as it infiltrated every society on earth, and for eternity.

My point is that many are called to become disciples, as opposed to being mere members of the multitude, but few actually respond. This is not to say that those who fail to choose the higher calling lose their salvation. I mean that when God calls a man or woman to become more than a consumer, more than just a believer among the multitude, when He calls him or her to a higher calling to serve and lead others, He brings that person under a training program designed to expose and break every fleshly confidence and every hidden sin. *That* is the dark night of the soul. Not mere burnout. Not exhaustion. It goes deeper than that and it requires an embracing of the wilderness untinged with anger or frustration.

Few are chosen because many abort the process in anger or despair before it can run its course. The price in suffering is simply too high. Those who opt out in order to rejoin the multitude are still saved and still redeemed; faith in Jesus assures the fact of their salvation, no matter what its level or intensity, but the loss of destiny and the aimlessness which result from such an abandonment of calling are grievous things to see. Those who won't take the cross can't take the calling.

In our day, God is refining a generation of leaders and servants in the crucible of brokenness, in the dark night of their souls. If you're part of this, there's a possible profile that I think may identify you. You've felt in your heart, perhaps for a long time, that God has some great thing for you to do, and maybe the early days of your ministry were powerfully anointed and successful, but lately you've been held back. Often, you've been forced to watch from the sidelines while others with less gifting or less wisdom than your own have been blessed and prospered of God. You've agonized over the question of why. You've felt wounded and left out, even rejected, and have then accused yourself for the jealousy you've known to be illegal.

It's likely that not much in your life has been less than a struggle for quite some time. Disaster has been a dominant theme for months, or even years. Major setbacks have piled one upon another. Disappointment threatens to crush the life and drive the hope from your heart and spirit. Or maybe you simply carry a burden of desperate hurt and agonizing loneliness that seems to have no cause or reason. Your dark night may be characterized more by an *inner* desolation than by any measurable *outward* set of circumstances. Out of this desolation, you've wondered tearfully and, perhaps angrily, where God is. Even your prayers seem to go nowhere. All of this may seem similar to burnout symptoms, but it goes much deeper.

Like so many of us, it may be that great things have been prophesied over you by those known for the accuracy of their words, but the only prophecies you've actually seen come to pass are the ones predicting disaster. You've been confused and hurt by that. *Why has the Lord dealt with me in this way?* He has dealt with you in this way because first He promises you and then He prepares you, and the heart of the preparation is brokenness.

It would have been a tremendous help if someone somewhere among God's people had given you a theological grid for understanding what has come upon you, but our faith has been too conditioned by the values and demands of the pagan society in which we live. In the eyes of the church, your experience of suffering is illegal, of the devil. No one ever told you that your call to discipleship would be a blessing preceded by a crucifixion - to be followed by a resurrection.

Why is this deep crushing so necessary? *Because our own strength, what we've known in the past, will not sustain us in the glory into which God is taking us.* We need a transcendent level of compassion, and an unthreatenable sense of peace under fire, in order to deal with the depth of destruction growing up around us in the world we're called to reach. If we're to save, heal and disciple a multitude out of this world's lostness, then we need a "loaves and fishes" kind of multiplication of the compassion and power of Jesus. Our pitifully and woefully inadequate offering of service will need to be miraculously multiplied by the hand of God.

In the unbroken believer, the natural capacity of the individual serves to limit and restrict the flow of God's compassion and power through that individual. In our natural selves, we are completely inadequate for the task of ministry or for the glory set before us, but in the weakness in which the power of God is perfected, Jesus multiplies the little we can offer and glorifies Himself far beyond what we ourselves could have produced (II Corinthians 12). In godly brokenness, grace and power flow unhindered and unlimited by the flesh.

Furthermore, our present level of holiness is

not sufficient to protect us where God is taking us. The glory and anointing of God are a blessing, but also a weight and pressure needing a solid foundation on which to rest. As the anointing increases, so does the spiritual pressure which tests and strains our character, and so does the accountability God demands of us. The weight of God's glory and anointing resting on a person must ultimately force open and reveal every crack and fissure in his or her inner self, every unholy ambition, every self-seeking impulse, every control mechanism, every unhealthy need, every immorality.

At first, this inner condition is exposed only to ourselves and to God, but if we turn away, seeking to avoid or deny His dealings, then our Lord makes our issues public. I could include a long list of names we'd all recognize as cases in which, as a last resort, God went public with a man's hidden sin in order to break him and draw him home again. Given a choice between saving a ministry and saving a person, our Lord will choose the person every time, so intensely does He love and desire us.

In His mercy and by means of the crucible of the cross, God is exposing our sin in order to reveal and humble us so that, under the weight of the glory to come, we'll be able to stand.

> **For everyone who does evil hates the light, and does not come to the light, lest his deeds should be exposed. But he who practices the truth comes to the light, that his**

deeds may be manifested as having been wrought in God. John 3:20-21.

We'll need a deeper holiness of the heart and a deeper river of compassion to enable us to stand in the wondrous places our Lord will take us in the days to come. For this reason, God has been dealing with His chosen vessels, grinding them to powder so fine it will float on water, as I once heard a man with a well-known prophetic ministry say. He went on to point out that when limestone is crushed and moistened with the water of the Holy Spirit, concrete is made. Weakness becomes strength. Our wise and compassionate God is leading us into the mystery of the experience of the apostle Paul.

And because of the surpassing greatness of the revelations, for this reason, to keep me from exalting myself, there was given me a thorn in the flesh, a messenger of Satan to buffet me - to keep me from exalting myself! Concerning this I entreated the Lord three times that it might depart from me. And he has said to me, "My grace is sufficient for you, for power is perfected in weakness." Most gladly, therefore, I will rather boast about my weaknesses, that the power of Christ may dwell in me.

144

Therefore I am well content with weaknesses, with insults, with distresses, with persecutions, with difficulties, for Christ's sake; for when I am weak, then I am strong. II Corinthians 12:7-10.

These verses are impenetrable to those conditioned by the health, wealth and prosperity gospel arising out of the materialistic society in which we live. **Was given me**, quoted in the passage above, is in the "divine passive" in the original Greek, meaning that the thorn, the **messenger of Satan**, was given to Paul *by God*. God Himself sent Paul a messenger of Satan in order to accomplish and maintain a state of weakness and brokenness in His servant. Paradoxically, by leaving Paul weak and unhealed, by placing him in a position that forced him to trust, God magnified the power He was able to pour through him in ministry to others and in ministry to him personally. **When I am weak, then I am strong.** No matter how talented or brilliant the minister, that which is limited by the flesh can never match what flows freely in the Spirit. Three times Paul cried out for healing and three times God refused. It wasn't that his faith was insufficient or that his life was filled with obvious sin. It was that God needed a broken vessel through which to pour out His miracles of loaves and fishes, miraculously multiplying His mercy for thousands who would hear Paul's message and receive his ministry. And he needed someone who would

145

remain utterly humble through it all.

God's grace to Paul was to show him unfathomable power and reveal to him unspeakable secrets and then break him in pieces before he could be prideful about it. And He left him that way. If Paul had been allowed power in himself, he would have been full of himself, full of ambition, striving and control, rather than full of Jesus. The result would not have been true faith, but a cult based on personality.

I myself thought that as I grew older in the Lord and grew closer to Him, I'd feel ever holier and cleaner. Exactly the opposite has been true. I have become ever more aware of how incomplete I am, how broken and destroyed by sin. The result has not been discouragement or heaviness. Instead, I'm filled with a growing and joyous awareness of the infinite magnitude of God's grace toward me. That's a place I can rest in.

In the midst of watching my life fall apart, God began to hold me up to the "holiness mirror". When in use, the holiness mirror seems to be positioned about two inches from the end of my nose so that I can't escape being faced with my own reflection, no matter which way I turn, and so that my own image is all I'm able to see. In short, in brokenness God makes us face ourselves.

One of the most difficult things for me to confront and absorb was the realization that I had spent most of my ministry full of myself and that while I was full of myself, the grace and mercy of God insured that not one single prophetic promise anyone ever spoke over my personal life came to pass. Unless it involved suffering. All of those prophecies were fulfilled.

This was God's mercy because I couldn't have sustained His destiny for me from where I was. The foundation was cracked. If I had achieved the success and acclaim promised by those prophetic words before *pathema* had done its work, I'd have patted myself on the back and gone off to teach others how to manipulate the principles of God to obtain spiritual success. That wasn't what Jesus wanted.

What God is doing with a great many of us isn't about manipulating principles. It's about power perfected in weakness. The new leadership is being trained in weakness and brokenness, and will therefore be immeasurably powerful. They'll lead boldly *when* Jesus is leading boldly, and *because* Jesus is leading boldly, not from a root in selfish ambition or the need for self-validation. Their heart's cry will be nothing more than to be where Jesus is. Only the power*less* can be truly *em*powered.

God is raising a generation of compassionate shepherds and leaders, but to produce His kind of compassion, He must take out the ambition, the hunger for power, the religion, the legalism, the control mechanisms, the unbelief and the judgment, all of which are often hidden in a myriad of subtle ways and places.

All my life, personal strength has been important to me. My Osage Indian ancestors (my father's side of the family) worshiped strength and size. Strength is written into my genetic code at levels so deep I have trouble separating myself from it in any way. In my flesh I long for and seek after emotional, physical and spiritual strength. Most of my life, until the dark night, has been consumed with the quest for that power.

Externally, I grew up in a power atmosphere. My father is a minister and, as far as I know, we were the first family to come into the charismatic movement in our old mainline denomination in 1958. Demons were cast out regularly in our living room. We battled them in the night in hand to hand combat, casting them away as they came to attack us. As a matter of course, people were miraculously healed both emotionally and physically in my parents' ministry, while I looked on in wonder.

My earliest memory of my father praying, other than saying grace over meals, is of walking past his room late one night and hearing him inside blissfully yammering away in tongues. As a child, I coveted that gift, not because it would bring me into a new intimacy with God, but because it represented power to me at a time when the world made me feel power*less.*

Later, as an adult with seven years of higher education behind me, I tried to build a powerful church and a powerful ministry. I worked at cultivating a powerful persona. I hungered for personal strength and spiritual power to heal, power to teach, power to lead, power to persuade.

Personally, I was a fleshly dynamo, a driven

man, contemptuous of those who couldn't keep pace with me. In the spirit, however, there was little experience of the power of God for me as an individual, no overwhelming experiences. Others were slain in the Spirit, but not me. Others were overcome, but not me. Others felt the Spirit of God through me, but I always felt personally cheated, jealous of those who did experience those things.

One day in the midst of my whining over my lack of that kind of experience (something I'm good at), the Lord confronted me with one of the more portentous questions of my life. "Which would you rather have? Foolish power or powerful wisdom?" Having read of King Solomon, I knew the answer and rightly chose wisdom, but I was a fool. I was a fool, not because the choice wasn't right (it was), but because I had no clue what price the getting of wisdom would exact from me. Knowledge comes from study, but wisdom comes only through suffering. God is raising a generation of wise leaders. But even as I came to understand the price of my choice, I was even more a fool because I didn't know that when I was all broken, I'd still be a fool. I'd just be a fool for Him.

God asked me another question. "Would you be willing to be the cause of healing and wholeness for many if no one ever knew it was you?" Would I be willing to set others in motion and see them praised for what I started? I said yes, and answered rightly, because I knew what was expected of me, but again I was a fool. I was a fool because I didn't have a clue what I was asking for or what the lesson would extract from me while I learned it. I would have to die. I would have to let go, but only by having my fingers slowly and painfully pried from the controls of my life and ministry, one at a time, by Someone a great deal stronger than I. More importantly, I would have to learn to rest in that powerlessness.

When I had finally become too weak to argue or maintain my defenses, when life's nightmare and the Lord's apparent absence had taken their toll, God began to show me myself as I really was. I came to understand that if my Lord didn't graciously reduce me to a weakness like Paul's, and if He didn't continue to do so, I would never see what He wanted me to see. Strong in myself, I'd be blind.

I thought I'd been building God's kingdom, but I saw that I was chasing success and running on ambition, using the Spirit of God to advance my personal agenda in the building of my ministry. I thought I'd been challenging people to serve God, but I was serving the god of my own self-validation, manipulating people to serve the idol of my ambition. I mouthed glory to God, but I hungered to be seen.

"Lord, I just want to serve you!" I cried, protesting my innocence, "Why is all this evil happening to me?"

The answer came immediately, "Yes, but you also want to be important, so you serve yourself."

"Lord, I only want to minister to people and see them healed." That was marvelously pious and - I thought - true.

"Yes, but you also want to feel My power as a

means to validate yourself and you want the people to be healed and 'behave' so that you can look good."

"Lord, I just want the people to evangelize." I was beginning to weaken, so this one wasn't so loudly spoken.

"Yes, but you also want the biggest church in town so you can feel secure. AND YOU'VE BEEN ANGRY WHEN I WOULDN'T COOPERATE!"

I couldn't understand why my friends, who had built the church with me from the earliest days, were leaving me, or why my church had seemed to become so lifeless. In my weakness, I came to see that it was my fault, that I had driven people away with my intensity, ambition and controlling nature born of unbelief. The revelation of my dysfunction was devastating, and the more so because I knew that no matter how hard I tried, I couldn't make myself change. The patterns were too deeply ingrained and I'd been subconsciously reinforcing them for much too long. I didn't know the difference between the real me and the persona I had built for projecting to the public. God Himself had to break the pattern. I would have to die.

God is not seeking a new accumulation of knowledge for this generation. His goal is character formation at the cross, death leading to life, the broken heart and spirit He doesn't despise. Purified motives make purified lives and ministries. Purified motives come only from brokenness. When I am weak, then He is strong.

There remains therefore a Sabbath

rest for the people of God. For the one who has entered His rest has himself also rested from his works, as God did from His. Hebrews 4:9-10.

God is bringing us to the end of our own works, and of our own ways of doing His works. In and through the Sabbath rest of the broken heart and spirit, He will do mighty things among us.

Therefore, since Christ has suffered in the flesh, arm yourselves also with the same purpose, because he who has suffered in the flesh has ceased from sin, so as to live the rest of the time no longer for the lusts of men, but for the will of God. I Peter 4:1-2.

Out of this weakness whose true name is strength, flows the clean and pure mercy of Jesus for which the lost and wounded hunger so desperately. We are going to be a people of mercy.

11
THE WILDERNESS

We live in a culture trained to avoid suffering at all costs. We have no paradigm for dealing with it, no framework by which to process it. Suffering frightens us. After initial demonstrations of compassion, even the church, which should be the agent of mercy, often retreats in fear from those who suffer relentlessly and inexplicably. Condemnation of the sufferer usually follows close behind. *You didn't have enough faith. You were in sin. This is happening to you **because** of you. You haven't prayed hard enough, worked hard enough, given enough. You're reaping something you've sown.*

Because of our fearful inability to deal with the wilderness experience, we often reject it, but, scripturally, the wilderness plays an essential role in our lives and callings. In fact, the wilderness is an indispensable prerequisite for truly high calling. Before being released into the fullness of their callings, each of the prophets and apostles was driven into some form of personal wilderness that prepared him for service. The whole nation of Israel, in fact, wandered forty years in the desert to be trained in readiness to take the promised land. They had been given a high calling as a people, but unbelief stood in the way. They still thought like slaves - Egypt was still too close behind them - but God needed a free people to take the land of Canaan. The character and integrity of Israel, as a people, needed to be refined and cleansed before they would have the faith to take the promised land or the strength to sustain its blessing.

God *must* deal deeply with the character and integrity of the one He calls. The heart of that dealing is to strip away all fleshly structures in order to expose the places of unbelief. I still find it a wonder that through all the devastations and near disasters, God never let me slip. No matter how bad things looked or felt, I can see with 20/20 hindsight that He held me firmly, preserved and kept me. And I can see the goodness, the greater purpose, emerging. I'm beginning to enjoy the faith and trust I've longed for all my life.

We are coming into a period of history when nothing will suffice for the character of those who lead but the true heart and nature of Jesus for His people. That nature never abuses, never manipulates and never violates. *The root of all spiritual and ecclesiastical abuse is unbelief*, personal insecurity, the need for self-validation. If I don't trust God for my place and position in this world, if my sense of His favor upon me is in question, if I fear personal rejection, then I will seek to build a world of control or achievement around my flaws to anesthetize my feelings or to cover up my tender places, and I will sooner or later end up badly using both people and the church to accomplish place, position and self-protection.

Until the deep reaches of the heart of insecurity and unbelief are broken - with its structures of control and ambition - none of us are safe to wield the power of God or walk in the fullness of His calling. The wilderness is the place of suffering and loss designed to accomplish this brokenness in the deep reaches.

In Psalm 63, in the wilderness of Judah, King David cried out, v.1, **O God, Thou art my God; I shall seek *Thee* earnestly;** *not* I shall seek the latest techniques of spiritual warfare to defeat my enemy, *not* I shall find out how to multiply the nation, *not* how do I increase my power, *not* how do I overcome adversity, or increase my prosperity, but, **I shall seek *Thee* earnestly.**

Wilderness fire consumes our personal agendas until we cease to see God as a means to an end and are reduced at last to just one hunger, one longing, *My soul thirsts for Thee*, **my flesh yearns for Thee, In a dry and weary land where there is no water.**

David's cry was, *I can find no refreshment in this desert. I can no longer even sense Your presence, Lord. So hungry am I for you that the longing of my soul has become a physical thing felt even in the flesh of my body. Please, Lord, just let me be with you. Nothing else matters.*

The next verse is worded very curiously, **Thus I have beheld Thee in the sanctuary, To see Thy power and Thy glory.** David was saying, ***Because I have been in the desert, because I am thirsty and weary and broken, I have beheld Thee.*** Not through prosperity or success or power, but through the experience of the desert, the time when there was no prosperity or success or power, David beheld his God. ***THE FUNCTION OF***

155

THE WILDERNESS IS TO STRIP AWAY EVERY AMBITION, EVERY ACCOMPLISHMENT, EVERY ABILITY OF THE FLESH TO ACHIEVE, EVERY SINFUL HABIT OF THE HEART, UNTIL NOTHING IS LEFT BUT A DESPERATE CRAVING HUNGER FOR THE PRESENCE OF JESUS and then, *when there is no other hunger*, the revelation comes. The wilderness makes you simple and sets you at rest with your God in simple purity.

Verse 3, **Because Thy lovingkindness is better than life, My lips will praise Thee.** In the wilderness you despair of life. Success, building a great church, getting promoted at work, being recognized for what you do, or being adored by your wife or husband, fade to insignificance next to longing after God. His lovingkindness, His touch and His presence become your singular consuming hunger.

Verse 5, **My soul is satisfied as with marrow and fatness, And my mouth offers praises with joyful lips.** *I'm weary. I'm hungry. Thirsty. Alone. I have nothing, but I've become rich. I'm fulfilled. Reduced to just one need, one hunger, and so I've beheld my God as I could not have beheld Him before, and it's enough for me.*

Verse 8, **My soul clings to Thee...** This was the king speaking, but, for all his power, like a frightened and helpless child he clung tightly to his God. After the wilderness, more than ever before, he knew he was just a man, not powerful, not wise and not important. Without strength, defenseless and broken, his soul clung to the Lord, no longer concerned with power, wisdom or importance, but only the embrace of his God.

At that point real faith comes. Verse 9, **But those who seek my life to destroy it, Will go into the depths of the earth.** v.10, **They will be delivered over to the power of the sword; They will be a prey for foxes.** Verse 11, **but** *the king will rejoice in God...* Not in how mighty he'd become, and not in all the right decisions he'd made or the prosperity that had come to him, but in God he would find his joy.

The wilderness had broken through layers of mistrust and unbelief to expose and cleanse his fear. Restfully now, he knew his God would fight for him, provide for him, do good for him.

Extended wilderness deprivation, loneliness, hunger, wandering and emptiness put you in touch with the only hunger that ever really matters. Because the wilderness crucifies all other desires but to be with your God, it makes you a safe leader who won't abuse, whether you're a leader in your church, in the world or only at home. The wilderness prepares you to walk safely in destiny and blessing without polluting it with sin or human agenda.

God may delay your destiny, your life's blessing or your fulfillment (a mate, a calling, the place of your anointing, what you were created to do, your prosperity) because He knows you'd trash it at this stage in your development. Your character isn't yet prepared to sustain the weight of it, so He holds the blessing in trust against that day when the wilderness has done its work.

The watchword for leaders today is Ezekiel 34.

> v.2, **Son of man, prophesy against the shepherds of Israel. Prophesy and say to those shepherds, "Thus says the Lord God, 'Woe, shepherds of Israel *who have been feeding themselves!* Should not the shepherds feed the flock?** v.3, **You eat the fat and clothe *yourselves* with the wool, you slaughter the fat sheep without feeding the flock.** v.4, **Those who are sickly you have not strengthened, the diseased you have not healed, the broken you have not brought back, nor have you sought for the lost; but *with force and with severity you have dominated them.*** v.5, **And they were scattered for lack of a shepherd, and they became food for every beast of the field and were scattered.** v.6, **My flock wandered through all the mountains and on every high hill and My flock was scattered over all the surface of the earth; and there was no one to search for**

them.'" v.7, Therefore, you shepherds, hear the word of the Lord. v.8, "As I live," declares the Lord God, "surely because My flock has become a prey, My flock has even become food for all the beasts of the field for lack of a shepherd, and My shepherds did not search for My flock, but rather *the shepherds fed themselves and did not feed My flock;* v.9, therefore, you shepherds, hear the word of the Lord: v.10, Thus says the Lord God, "Behold, I am against the shepherds, and I shall demand My sheep from them and make them cease from feeding sheep. So the shepherds will not feed themselves any more, but I shall deliver My flock from their mouth, that they may not be food for them.

I believe a great many current leaders of the flock are about to be relieved of duty so that God can give the flock into the care of others who will follow after His own heart and not after their own ambitions. He is raising a generation of wilderness-trained shepherds, men and women who have walked the dark night of the soul and come out the other side, who will bring a new/old thing to the body of Christ, and He's training a people to walk with them, a people who together will look like Him, who'll be that bride that brings honor to His name, in all her glory without spot or wrinkle.

The wilderness is a place of testing.

Deuteronomy 8:2-3, **And you shall remember all the way which the Lord your God has led you in the wilderness these forty years,** *that He might humble you,* _testing_ **you, to** _know what was in your heart_**, whether you would keep His commandments or not.** *And He humbled you* **and let you be hungry, and fed you with manna which you did not know, nor did your fathers know,** *that He might make you understand that man does not live by bread alone but man lives by everything that proceeds out of the mouth of the Lord.*

Will you stand firm with the Lord in the midst of the humbling and testing of your heart? No matter what comes, will you love Him? Serve Him? Praise Him? Will you do it no matter how your situation looks? No matter how dry or distant He seems? Whether things go right or wrong? The truth is that if you can't stand for and with Him when everything seems wrong, then how shallow and cheap will your service be in the midst of blessing and prosperity?

After the wilderness, you no longer argue with God. A key part of the test is, **whether**, under the worst of circumstances, **you will keep His commandments.** You no longer ask, "Does obedience *work?*" Whether you can perceive that it works or not, you simply obey for the sake of being with Him. Wilderness stripping and wilderness testing establish your faith on a base of pure hunger for the Lord and His will, without dispute or compromise. Make a place in your theology for long periods of failure and humiliation which are designed to break down interior walls that hinder intimacy with Him.

God will humiliate you in the very areas He plans to bless you, in order to prepare you for the blessing. My old church in Idaho refused to grow. Now I'm at New Song Fellowship in Denver, which is a church of 500+ in an area of the city where, until very recently, every church plant but us has failed over the last five years. I'm a gifted musician and songwriter, but my music was shut off and hidden in Idaho. When I first came to Denver, I endured some ridicule by fellow musicians in the mega-church where I was executive pastor for fourteen months. Most doors seemed closed. New Song now owns its own recording studio while invitations to do the music outside our church are increasing. Last summer we signed a five album recording contract with a record label. Integrity is everything to me, but at the first church I served in Denver, my honor was trashed, my integrity questioned and slanderous lies were spread concerning me. Now God is vindicating me wherever I go.

You're a prophet? No one wants to hear your words. You're not even very accurate at first. You're a teacher? No one comes to your class. You're a family destined for blessing? Then why does everything seem all wrong all the time? You're a businessman destined for prosperity? You're broke and nothing you do succeeds as it should! *We must be reduced to a state in which we receive honor and humiliation with equal gratitude because we've been reduced to a simple singular hunger where all that matters is the presence and the love of Jesus.*

The desert is a place where you learn who you are and become established in it. In Matthew 3 and 4, Jesus came up from the waters of baptism with the Holy Spirit on Him and was driven immediately to the wilderness *in order to be tempted by the devil.* Those called of God will be tempted by the devil in ways actually commissioned by God.

The heart of it for Jesus was Matthew 4:3 and 6, *If* **you are the Son of God.** The key word is **if.** Satan sought for an exploitable window of insecurity or doubt in Jesus concerning His identity. Jesus' answers established Him in obedience to His Father and spoke of His identity, that He would do nothing but what He heard and saw His Father doing. **Man shall not live by bread alone...,** v.4, and v.7, **you shall not put the Lord your God to**

162

the test.   v.10, **you shall worship the Lord your God and serve Him only.** The temptation in the wilderness sharpened in Jesus a singular hunger for His Father's fellowship that reduced all earthly rewards to insignificance. I believe He came out of it knowing more fully His own place, who He was as the Son, and who His Father was, and that He would rise to no ambition that would endanger the relationship.   After forty wilderness years of weeding out unbelief and disobedience, the people of Israel knew who they were and who their God was. With that faith and that secure identity established, they conquered and held their promised land.

I lost a great many years not really knowing who I was, not really understanding or believing my chosenness. Because of an old root of rejection, I couldn't really believe God favored me. I therefore built a fortress of ambition and achievement around the absence of that knowledge and even became an abusive leader trying to maintain enough success around me that I wouldn't have to face my sense of rejection and my fear of it. The wilderness burned rejection out of me, revealed my God to me and set my hunger in order.

The desert can be a place of rest. Jesus said to the disciples, **Come away by yourselves to a lonely place and rest a while** (Mark 6:31). This may sound backwards to our acculturated ears, but we must to learn to rest in the pain, to rest in the loneliness and to plumb the depths of hunger and thirst. Yield to it and let it work its work. It is the hand of a loving God doing good for us. He wants more than our service; He wants *us*. In fact, if He must choose between you and your service, He will choose you every time. Given a choice between the ministry and the man, our Lord saves the man. He can raise up a ministry at a mere word, but a man is a precious, eternal and beloved son.

I carry a bit of that wilderness, my dark night of the soul, within me all the time, almost as a fragrance or an echo in my spirit of the path I walked. It reminds me who I am and teaches me wisdom. The wilderness has become a place of peace in the midst of the pressures of the ministry, a place where I remember my own weakness and God's strength, that God is my provider, a place where I cling to that singular hunger for the pure presence of my Lord. I go back there - or am taken there - whenever my cleansing needs to go deeper, or whenever I have gotten off the track in some way.

Ministry itself becomes a place of rest after the wilderness. The dark night of the soul brings about the end of self-motivated efforts and the solidifies the realization that only the sovereignty of God brings true blessing. Not my talent. Not my ability. Not *my* anointing. The anointing isn't mine anyway.

In the wilderness I came to realize that no matter how good I was, it was nothing if God didn't bless. I could be the best preacher, the best teacher, the most skilled administrator and the wisest pastor, but if God Himself didn't anoint it, there would be no fruit. I've seen God anoint fools and scoundrels to great ministry and set wise men on the sidelines simply because of His sovereignty and mercy.

THE WILDERNESS IS THEREFORE THE PLACE WHERE GOD BLESSES BY NOT BLESSING SO THAT YOU LEARN WHAT YOU CAN*NOT* DO and come to rest in Him. He sustains us in the wilderness but holds back the promise, just as Israel was sustained by Him in its corporate wilderness, but was held back from the promised land until the changed character of the people could bear the blessing.

> *The wilderness is a place of restoration.*
> Hosea 2:14-15, **Therefore, behold, I will allure her, Bring her into the wilderness, And speak kindly to her. Then I will give her vineyards from there And the valley of Achor as a door of hope.**

After the cleansing fire, after the hurt, after the judgment on my sin, when I have come to that singular hunger for the pure presence of Jesus, then I am ready for what the Lord intended for me all along. I am safe for it. I will wield it effectively for the Lord's bride and not destroy it through flesh or foolishness.

The foundation must go deeper for the building to go higher. The wilderness digs and lays the foundation for all that must come later. Therefore, for a great work, God digs a deep hole. He is more concerned with forming your character than He is with building a great ministry, more concerned with what adversity produces in you than with delivering you from it.

In the wilderness the Lord began to grant me the character changes I had asked for all my life. In the wilderness He restored me to myself and to Him when I had become lost in fear, striving, ambition and control.

The desert is a place of preparation.

Isaiah 40:3-5, **A voice is calling, "Clear the way for the Lord in the wilderness; Make smooth in the desert a highway for our God. Let every valley be lifted up, And every mountain and hill be made low; And let the rough ground become a plain, and the rugged terrain a broad valley; Then the glory of the Lord will be revealed, And all flesh will see it together; For the mouth of the Lord has spoken."**

Clear the way *in the wilderness, in the desert* a highway for our God. Prepare for His coming by taking out of the highway the obstructions, lumps and bumps. The wilderness removes impediments to the Lord's coming in your life by reducing you to that place where God alone will satisfy and where you've given up seeking satisfaction anywhere else. It is a state in which being with Him is more important than success, in which personal need and fear don't pollute what you do. Without a preparatory wilderness there can be no promised land, no destiny.

The wilderness can present dangers. There are pitfalls and traps that hook us in our bad theology or in our tendencies to walk in the flesh, rather than by the Spirit of God. Forewarned is forearmed, and so I list some of those dangers here.

__Anger and bitterness__: Does God expect me to embrace this experience with no bitterness? In the end, yes He does. I've learned that if you still have the strength to be angry with God concerning your suffering, then you have some distance yet to go. Seek God for grace to surrender without bitterness.

Over the years, I've grown so tired of judging God for His dealing with me that most of the time anymore I simply don't have the energy for it. Israel in the wilderness was an angry people until anger was burned and bred out of them. In the face of every new obstacle they rose up to grumble and complain against Moses and God, no matter how many miracles of deliverance God had led them through. God is good and intends only good for us. Wounding by His hand is an act of love designed to prepare us for the goodness of our destiny by refining the foundation of our character until real faith takes form in our hearts.

__Erosion of faith__: Isn't it ironic that the thing designed to scour out of me my fleshly impediments to faith could actually result in the loss of it? There was a time when I knew for certain that the favor of God was not with me and that there was nothing I could do to restore it. For that period of time I was right. It was my wilderness, my dark night of the soul. The faith problem surfaced when God had accomplished in me what He had set out to accomplish and I found myself unable to transition out of the wilderness into believing God for the blessing. It was time for favor to return, but I was stuck in the wilderness mentality, believing that God didn't want to bless me and that He never really would.

This thinking is recognizable by the phrases it produces. *It is **always** this way... This **always** happens... God will **never**...* The truth is that the wilderness itself was a blessing that prepared me for the greater blessing yet to come, but wilderness thinking and wilderness unbelief can render me incapable of believing for it or of recognizing it when it arrives.

Part of what God was exposing was my bitter root expectancy that I would always have to fight my battles alone. My judgment on life and God was that, in the face of real obstacles, I'd always be on my own. I developed that judgment on life and God while growing up with my father. Always, when the chips were down, I fought my battles alone without him. I therefore couldn't believe my Father God would back me up or fight for me. It led to fear and striving and not a little domination and control of the people who walked with me.

When God let things come unravelled in my life in order to expose that thing in me, I concluded that it was all happening again, that I was once again fighting for my life without real help, and so I despaired. When it was time for favor to return, I had to work through it, repenting of the judgment and seeking healing, because it was time to choose to have faith again, to believe that my Father God would, indeed, fight for me. And He did.

What if my expectation had hardened and my bitterness had become permanent, as it was with that first generation of Israelites in the wilderness? How much blessing, how many promised lands, might I have locked out? I have a God who loves me. In love He disciplined me in the wilderness to expose my character flaws by leaving me to fight more battles on my own than I could handle in my flesh, *so that I would break* and so that unbelief would be refined out of my character. But when His purpose had been accomplished, He restored His favor over me and I was required to choose to believe again. *In truth, all of it had been an expression of His favor.* He had loved me enough to risk me in order to save me.

There is real danger of **_apostasy_** in the wilderness. *I've had enough. I'm bailing out. I didn't have these problems before I was a believer! Jesus doesn't work. I'll quit or I'll opt for a lesser level of Christianity.* Jesus said that many are called and few are chosen. This attitude is one reason why few are chosen.

Rebellion may take root. *I'll fix you! See if I pray to You! I'll just go rent a few porno movies and see how you like that! I just won't talk to you for a while, so there!* You may have said or felt these things. Or perhaps God has said no to a ministry you want to do, but you're determined to do it anyway. For instance, God had set up my church in Idaho to behave in just the way that would expose my flaws and eventually move me away to Denver. I tried to escape the pain by planting an extension congregation 20 miles away in Spokane. I did one service in Idaho and one in Spokane every Sunday. I expected it to grow and make me feel better, but it didn't grow, and I was forced to close it several months later. Because He loves me, God refused to bless my effort to circumvent His plan. Don't ask Him to bless your efforts to circumvent His plan for you.

In the wilderness, _disobedience_ carries a certain appeal. At one point God told me to pray morning and evening to bracket the day in prayer during a time of crisis. I could have refused, but I know the crisis would then have escalated. God told me to publicly make amends to the elders of our church in Idaho for my use and abuse of them. What if I'd said no? Or what if I'd quit my ministry? Blessings would have been lost and character changes would have been delayed. Many confused wilderness leaders do opt out. What tragedy! What loss!

Turning to other powers is always out of bounds. Those other powers might be fleshly strength and talent, personal charm or force of will to persuade others. They might be domination and control. They might be compromise with new age techniques. I might resort to intimidation. I've seen the Holy Spirit send men to the wilderness by letting decline happen in their ministries, but instead of embracing the sufferings, they turned to domination, condemnation and control of their people in order to try to hold it all together. Or lies and deceptions were used to push the "empire" forward. Dishonest fund-raising tactics and hype are often part of the repertoire. In the family, this same dynamic can manifest as anger, unreasonable demands, or emotional and/or physical withdrawal.

We can *seek relief*, counselor after counselor, conference after conference, new plan after new plan, but the only way out of the wilderness is *through* it. Wilderness is the preparation for promise. How long does it take? It takes as long as it takes. Can you shorten the journey? No, but you can make it longer. The difference between redemptive suffering and misery is whether you embrace it or fight it. The more you complain the longer God lets you live.

12
AWED BY THE MYSTERY

Job is probably the most difficult book of the Bible to work with, partly because of its complexity, and partly because its message is really difficult to hear. In a very few verses Job went from prosperity and happiness as a wealthy man honored and respected in his community, to absolute poverty and destruction. And God gave permission to Satan to make it happen. Job-like experiences often force us to question the fairness and justice of God's dealings with us. I no longer believe God ever promised us fairness this side of the return of Christ. He *did* promise He'd never leave us or forsake us. That's the part I've found to be absolutely reliable, no matter what my senses or emotions have told me. Before it was all over, no part of his (Job's) life had escaped the ruin. Justice was never the issue.

Urgency and fear on his sweating face, a messenger came running to Job with news that as the oxen plowed the fields and the donkeys grazed, raiders came, slew all the servants and made off with the animals. In modern terms we could say that an enemy had murdered his employees and stolen all his tools. Job was out of business. And his other enterprise? Raiders killed those servants, as well, and then took all his camels. In one devastating day, both his manufacturing and shipping operations had been wiped out and his financial empire laid waste.

I can imagine Job comforting himself, "Ah, but I still have my family," as another runner breathlessly approached. Between gasps, he reported that Job's sons and daughters had been enjoying their cycle of feasts in one another's homes when a sudden violent windstorm came up and collapsed the house. All Job's children died in the rubble. His life. His posterity. Those who would take care of him in his old age. His living retirement plan. Not only were those he loved dead, but neither would anyone be around to support him in his old age. I can only imagine how he must have felt as he searched through the ruins for the mangled bodies of his beloved children.

Being a righteous man, and having trained himself to turn to God in all things, **Job arose and tore his robe and shaved his head** (Jewish expressions of mourning) **and he fell to the ground and worshiped** (1:20). Lots of us would blame and punish God in the face of this kind of devastation. *See if I come to your church anymore. I'll just quit praying. See how you like that!* But Job was wholly absorbed in serving his Lord. I call it being *wholly owned*. So he stowed his feelings away and fell down and worshiped. He grew angrier later as worse disasters befell him and the pressures escalated, but for now he held it together and did the right religious thing.

> **And he said, "Naked I came from my mother's womb, And naked I shall return there. The Lord gave and the Lord has taken away. Blessed be the name of the Lord"**

(v.21). Through all this Job did not sin nor did he ascribe unseemliness to the Lord (v.22).

In other words, Job refused to accuse the Lord of being unfair or inappropriate. In all his wealth, he knew he'd never possessed anything but what the Lord had given him. He'd enjoyed it while he had it. Although he grieved his losses, he faithfully confessed the goodness of the Lord as good theology dictated that he should. He was a righteous man dealing with his grief in a righteous way. He grew angrier later, but this early in his long ordeal, he spoke the good with his mouth. How religiously and theologically correct!

Yet there was a great deal more for Job to absorb, and he was about to be tested beyond his ability to deal with it. Job had yet to be overwhelmed by his suffering. Grief and disaster can sometimes come so quickly, one blow on top of another, that they overwhelm our human capacity to cope. Suffering can sometimes become so intense and so relentless that we can no longer adequately process it. This was about to become Job's experience. He had been called by God. He had enjoyed his calling and anointing freely and without price, but he was about to enter a wilderness exile of suffering, after which he would be recalled into even greater prosperity and blessing than he had known before. More importantly, his relationship with God would move to a new plane.

He passed the first test so well that in chapter 2

God bragged on him. *"Isn't Job great? I'm so proud of him!"* But Satan pointed out that God had left him healthy and strong, claiming that if He would allow him to afflict Job's body and ruin his health, it would become readily and quickly apparent what he was *really* made of. He accused the Lord of protecting Job unduly and stated that without that protection, Job wouldn't serve God at all. In response, God removed the hedge of protection, and it wasn't long before Job was stricken with the most painful and disfiguring form of disease imaginable.

Boils appeared all over his body, injecting poison into his system and inflaming his nerves with unbearable pain. With the boils came a maddening itch. The infection so affected his appearance that people became disgusted at the very sight of him. Maggots began to hatch in the ulcerations as his skin began to blacken and peel. Terrible nightmares plagued him in his sleep. The Bible even mentions bad breath, as if to cast a final insult upon an already devastated beggar.

At last he made his pain-wracked way to the dung heap outside the city, where it was customary for those in mourning to roll in the ashes and throw dust in the air. It was a place for outcasts and expressions of extreme grief. There Job sat, hour after hour, scraping the puss from his boils with bits of broken pottery, and brooding over his fate. Water was sacred in that region of scarcity. It was therefore believed that the container that carried water was also holy, and that the broken pieces of a water pot contained healing properties because of that holiness. In short, Job was attempting to doctor himself in the only way left to him.

There on the dung heap, his wife came to mock him in her bitterness and loss, tempting him to curse God and die. He refused, and we hear nothing more of her. Job was left alone, his deprivations now complete.

Friends who came to commiserate found it difficult even to recognize his face and were stricken speechless at his appearance. For seven oppressive days they sat with him in the dust and dung, stunned to silence, speaking not a word. In chapter 3, Job finally broke. In mortal agony of body and soul he cursed the very day of his birth and moaned in despair, **I am not at ease, nor am I quiet, And I am not at rest, but turmoil comes** (v.26).

That kind of suffering frightens other believers. *How could God let all this disaster happen to someone who loves Him and serves Him so well, and if He could let it happen to Job, could He let it happen to me?* Because it threatened their sense of security, Job's friends couldn't face that possibility. As a result, they were driven by fear to theologize Job's suffering in order to gain a sense of control over the situation and to reassure themselves that it couldn't happen to them. Job's condition frightened them in the same way that senseless and relentless suffering frighten us today, and so, by way of offering comfort and counsel, they began to expound their theological understanding of why men suffer. Their arguments sound a great deal like some of the legalistic faith teaching we hear today in some parts of the body of Christ, and were every bit as destructive.

Because they had a mechanical view of the nature of God, Job's friends had no adequate theological framework for processing extended and overwhelming human suffering. Their thought was that if we would behave just so, God must bless us, or at least preserve us from serious harm. In that light, what was happening to Job made no sense to them. *You mean we can't control God?* So after seven days they began to preach, and they called it "comfort".

Eliphaz spoke first (chapter 4). Like a good many religious fools acting in the name of ministry, his offering of comfort included two of the most hurtful assumptions that can possibly be visited upon a sufferer. The first comes in verses 7 and 8:

Remember now, who ever perished being innocent? Or where were the upright destroyed? According to what I have seen, those who plow iniquity And those who sow trouble harvest it.

This is "formula faith" and it goes like this: God rewards righteousness and punishes the wicked; therefore all who suffer deserve it. Faith brings healing; therefore all who are not healed have failed in faith. God prospers those who give faithfully and deal honestly; therefore those who are poor have done some wrong thing to get that way.

177

If you believe rightly, act rightly, confess rightly and try hard enough, you will be well and prosperous. This was the theology of Job's day - it reflected their view of how to work the principles of God's law for personal benefit - and it has become a prominent theology in our own time. One of our oldest heresies, it reduces God to a set of mechanical principles and heaps guilt and condemnation on those He loves when their experience of life doesn't fit the mold. It takes the mystery out of the majesty of God and reduces Him to something our finite minds can effectively contain. It is an ancient, subtle and insidiously cruel system and I hate it with all my heart.

As if what he was already saying to Job weren't vicious enough, Eliphaz added the second element. I hear it often today.

> Verses 12-13, **Now a word was brought to me stealthily, And my ear received a whisper of it, Amid disquieting thoughts from the visions of the night when deep sleep falls on men, Then a spirit passed by my face; the hair of my flesh bristled up. It stood still but I could not discern its appearance; A form was before my eyes; There was silence, then I heard a voice.**

"I had a dream. GOD HIMSELF told me why you were suffering. Brother, I have a word for

you!" Eliphaz shaded the content of this word in tones of mystery so that Job would be both impressed and convinced, as if the fact that it came cloaked in mysticism meant it must be God. But what is mystical isn't always divine, and what is not divine can often deeply wound. The ultimate content of Eliphaz's "word from God" was, *You're suffering because you're guilty because righteous people never suffer these kinds of things.*

Job was being disciplined by God, he stated flatly (5:17-27). Job should simply submit and praise God and then everything would be restored. How nauseatingly simplistic! Confronted with this kind of spiritual excrement, Job's pained and angry reaction was both predictable and understandable.

> **Thou dost frighten me with dreams and terrify me by visions; So that my soul would choose suffocation, Death rather than my pains (7:14-15).**

Bildad is next. Chapter 8:5:

> **If you would seek God... v.6, If you are pure and upright, Surely now He would rouse Himself for you and restore your righteous estate...**

In other words, *Your devotional life sucks, Job. You need to pray more. If you would only pray more, He'd make you a good man again.*

The long and the short of the remainder of Bildad's argument is that because God cannot be unjust, Job must be suffering because of some great sin. If he'd only confess that sin, he'd be fine. These three were nothing if not consistent!

Job's rebuttal, in what had now become a great debate, was that evil men grow wealthy and they die in peace. If what Bildad says is true, how can that be? Shouldn't they suffer all these things as penalty for *their* sin, as well? Obviously, the universe doesn't always work the way Bildad believes it does. Job is therefore innocent, and, if he is innocent, how could he be suffering for some great sin? If suffering is always the punishment of God, why are the bad guys doing so well?

How many of us have believed God withholds our blessing because we've not been good enough? How many of us have heard it said that God *can't* bless us because there's sin in our lives? Well, if that's true, who qualifies for blessing? Which of us is sinless? And it seems to me that if we did actually qualify, we'd be perfect and in no need of a Savior. In fact, we *don't* qualify and that's *why* we need Jesus!

Bildad could write a book today that would probably sell a million copies. It's title would read something like <u>Prayers that Really Work: Five Certain Steps to Health and Happiness</u>. We could read it and get God in a box. We'd push all the right buttons and He would respond by doing everything we want so that we wouldn't have to live any longer with the mystery of suffering, the mystery of His nature, the mystery of His ways. Did we forget Isaiah 55:8-9?

"For my thoughts are not your thoughts, Neither are your ways My ways," declares the Lord. "For as the heavens are higher than the earth So are My ways higher than your ways, And My thoughts than your thoughts."

The religious spirit makes a formula out of our relationship with God and denies the unfathomable mystery. But how could the finite possibly hope to fathom the infinite? How could those whose power, perception and wisdom are limited by their creatureliness possibly fathom the purposes of the Almighty whose power, perception and wisdom are limited by nothing? How could we who know so little possibly comprehend the purposes and reasonings of Him who not only knows it all, but created all things from nothing and purposed all things from the beginning?

Whenever we lose sight of the mystery and begin to think we have God and life figured out, we've entered into a religious spirit, and wherever the religious spirit goes, cruelty is ever close at hand and people inevitably get hurt. Job's friends were cruel in their comfort. They'd lost sight of the mystery of God and had reduced His dealings to a mechanical set of principles they could control and be comfortable with. Senseless suffering was something for which they had no paradigm. The mystery of the nature and dealings of God were too threatening.

In a later chapter, Zophar began to speak, angry that Job would protest innocence. In Zophar's view, Job's punishment was less than he deserved because he refused to admit his guilt - which, in his view, was obviously present because he wouldn't have been suffering if he weren't guilty. If Job honestly didn't know what his sins were, then God certainly did, and the reason for the suffering was that God was awakening Job to repentance. Job was crushed.

God is not a formula. When we reduce our view of God's nature to a set of principles we can manipulate, we inevitably judge and destroy those whose experiences don't fit the formula. There's a whole generation of believers out there who've suffered in this way at the hands of those who thought they had it together. When a leader becomes too ensconced in his theology, too imprisoned in his comfortable understanding of how things work or how they ought to be done, he misses God and becomes an abuser. God's remedy, the corrective measure, is often a dark night of the soul, like Job's, that ultimately restores God servant to mercy, compassion, fellowship with God and a profound and humble appreciation for mystery.

Here's what Job himself knew. 1) He knew for certain that God was responsible for his suffering. At no time did he challenge or question that assumption and God Himself never corrected it. Job never attempted to split theological hairs or play word games over whether it was the direct hand of God or that God *allowed* Satan to do it. To him it was all God. 2) He knew there was no discernable reason for what had happened to him, nothing a human being could understand or attribute to some great principle. He knew he didn't *deserve* his suffering.

So he confronted his tormentors in 13:4-5:

...worthless physicians are you all.
Oh that you would keep silent and
it would be your wisdom! 19:2,
How long will you torment and
break me in pieces with words?

The kind of religion practiced by Job's friends takes the mystery out of the nature of God and reduces a living relationship to a formula. When that happens, the wounded are always abused. Arrogance is like that.

Job longed desperately to understand why God had done all this to him and he argued hurtfully with his friends who thought they had the answers and had solved the mystery. They had judged Job guilty. *He suffers; therefore he is guilty.*

Because sin does inevitably bear fruit in human suffering, sometimes we *can* legitimately work forward from sin to the suffering it produces, but one of the many lessons of the book of Job is that we can*not* always work backward from suffering to a *cause* in sin.

Actually, Job was trapped in the same religious spirit his friends were. This was part of his agony. Deeply and desperately he searched for some sin that would explain it all. I believe he *wanted* to find something, because it would have helped him understand, and because he would have been able to chart a course of action in repentance. But it wasn't there and he came up empty-handed, confronted with the impenetrable mystery of the purposes of God. The result was an even deeper despair. I know. I've been there.

In the end, because the formula wouldn't work and because understanding refused to come, Job became as angry with God as he had been with his friends. *I have done nothing to deserve this. I am righteous, yet I suffer horribly! I don't understand. It's not fair!* Sometimes mercy begins at the point of our own willingness to sit humbly before the mystery and say to God and to our brother, "I don't know."

For a time, God allowed Job to vent his anger over what he perceived as grossly unfair treatment. When at last God spoke, His words were a stunning rebuke to human understanding and to our pride in our capacity to comprehend. **The Lord answered Job out of the whirlwind and said, "Who is this that darkens counsel By words without knowledge?** (38:1-2). *You've spoken a lot of words and argued a lot of theology and made yourselves sound really intelligent, but you fools don't know what you're talking about.* Verse 3, **Now gird up your loins like a man** *(Stop* *whimpering, get off the pity pot!)*, **And I will ask you, and you instruct Me!** (divine sarcasm) Verse 4, **Where were you when I laid the foundations of the earth! Tell Me, if you have understanding?** Verse 5, **Who set its measurements since you know? Or who stretched the line on it?**

And God went on listing the mysteries of the universe, verse after verse. Verse 12, **Have you ever in your life commanded the morning?** There is the French story of "The Little Prince" who lived on a planet all his own and over which he was king. He claimed that so complete was his rule, and so powerful his reign, that he could actually command the sun to rise. When challenged to prove his sovereignty by doing so, he stated that the conditions were not yet right for obedience, that only at a certain time of the day were the conditions right for the sun to obey his command to rise. Such is both our human helplessness and our arrogance.

Is it by your understanding that the hawk soars? (39:26). What incredible effrontery to suppose that we could fathom the designs of God! Who do we think we are? To really *know* God is to be confronted with the impenetrable mystery. Get used to it! If you would walk with Him, then you must learn to live with unanswered questions - questions that the finite human mind could never hope to grasp the answer to, no matter how hard we might try or how long we might study.

Yet in our suffering we are often driven, as Job was, to cry out that God has been unfair toward us! We would pass judgment on His dealings! We would question the wisdom of what He allows to happen all because we presume to understand! This is precisely the point God comes to in Job 40:8, **Will you really annul My judgment? Will you condemn Me that you may be justified?** God hasn't been fair? God broke the contract? Do we really think we know better than He concerning the course of our lives and that we've gotten a "bum steer" out of it? Where were we when He called light into being or set the earth on its course? We do not and cannot understand. God is a permanent mystery with purposes for each of us that we couldn't possibly fathom. In fact, if He ever really tried to tell us what they were, or how He was going to bring them to pass, we'd remain profoundly confused and would probably end up more angry with him than before the explanation was given.

Our best modern minds are currently trying to understand how the universe came into being. For years we've been hearing about the "big bang" theory which proposes that the universe came about by means of a huge explosion that threw matter outward from the center. Now, new discoveries are surfacing concerning the placement of galaxies and the speed at which they travel that seem to invalidate that theory. The world of astronomy is in an uproar. Back to the mystery!

Thousands of galaxies are grouped in clusters around the known universe, and in them are uncounted stars at distances from us and from one another that reduce the human mind to helpless and hopeless confusion. But the awesome mystery is that God made it with a word - all of it - and He rules it by decree, knowing the movement of every atom of every bit of matter in every star system in every galaxy. What makes us think we can comprehend Him, much less judge His dealings or challenge His wisdom? We need a new revelation of the mystery and the awe of God, and the grace to rest in it.

42:1, **Then Job answered the Lord, and said, I know that Thou canst do all things, And that no purpose of Thine can be thwarted.** Job was beginning to get the point. *You're not limited by this stupid theology we humans have been discussing.* **Who is this that hides counsel without knowledge? Therefore I have declared that which I did not understand. Things too wonderful for me, which I did not know. Hear now and I will speak; I will ask Thee and do Thou instruct me.**

We must give up the human pride that enables us to be angry with God for what we think is unfair in the course of our lives. We must surrender to the mystery, even when it includes what we believe to be senseless suffering. The dark night has taught me some understanding, at least, of what the apostle Paul meant when he wrote:

> **...I have learned to be content in whatever circumstances I am. I know how to get along with humble means, and I also know**

**how to live in prosperity; in any
and every circumstance I have
learned the secret of being filled
and going hungry, both of having
abundance and suffering need. I
can do all things through Christ
who strengthens me.** Philippians
4:11-13.

Verse 5, **I have heard of Thee by the
hearing of the ear; But now my eye sees
Thee; v.6, Therefore I retract, And I repent
in dust and ashes.** Job repented for His
understanding of God, for believing he understood
what could not possibly *be* understood. At the end
of exile and pain, Job found his place again in the
scheme of things. Human pride had become divine
humility, and so he entered into a restored peace with
God, captivated by the mystery. God got out of the
box, and isn't that where we *really* want Him?
Standing eternally and lovingly above our ability to
control Him?

St. John of the Cross, teaching on the seven
mansions of the soul, spoke of the beatitude that came
after the dark night, a state of peace, joy and rest
with God that truly does pass understanding. My
own walk has brought me episodes of this at a level
I've never experienced before. Sometimes I have to
actively choose to stay there because my grip on that
state is often tenuous at best. I often fail, but it's
always there waiting for me to return. It has
revolutionized my dealing with people, my

preaching, my leadership and my handling of crises. My wife is delighted. She finds a resting place in me these days that she's never known in all our twenty-five years of marriage. She deserves it; she's waited a long time.

The end of the story is that Job's "formula faith" comforters were in big trouble with God, while Job himself became three times as prosperous and blessed as before. Having been captivated anew by the mystery, and having been humbled in his own understanding, he had become a safe repository for the real blessing God had stored up for him all along. How safe are you and I to receive our blessing, our calling, our destiny? How ready to occupy our promised land? Still judging God? Still thinking we really know? Still preaching great sermons to the suffering out of our ignorance and fear? I don't know. I only know there's a lot more to God and His goodness than we can ever learn of or even begin to fathom, and I think that's awesome!

BOOK ORDER FORM

To order additional copies of this book direct from the publisher, please use this order form. Also note that your local bookstore can order titles for you.

Book Title	Price	Quantity	Amount
BURNOUT: Renewal In The Wilderness	$10.95	_____	$_____

Total Book Amount $_____

Shipping & Handling - Add $1.95 for the *first* book, plus $0.50 for *each* additional book. $_____

TOTAL ORDER AMOUNT - Enclose check for money order (No cash or COD's) $_____

Make check or money order payable to: **EXANIMO CORPORATION**

Mail order to: **EXANIMO CORPORATION**
               P.O. Box 1110
               Concrete, WA 98237

Please print your name and address clearly:

Name: _____

Address: _____

City: _____

State or Province: _____

Zip or Postal Code: _____

Telephone Number: (____)_____

Foreign orders must be submitted in U.S. dollars. Foreign oders are shipped by uninsured surface mail. We ship all orders within 48 hours of receipt of order.

NOTE: A listing of other books, tapes, and music by Loren Sandford, and the New Song Worship Band can be obtained by writing to Exanimo Corporation. Add a request to your book order, or write for list.